Food Waste

Materializing Culture
Series Editors: Paul Gilroy and Daniel Miller

Food Waste

Home Consumption, Material Culture and Everyday Life

David Evans

B L O O M S B U R Y

LONDON • NEW DELHI • NEW YORK • SYDNEY

Bloomsbury Academic
An imprint of Bloomsbury Publishing Plc

50 Bedford Square	1385 Broadway
London	New York
WC1B 3DP	NY 10018
UK	USA

www.bloomsbury.com

Bloomsbury is a registered trade mark of Bloomsbury Publishing Plc

First published 2014

British Library Cataloguing-in-Publication Data
A catalogue record for this book is available from the British Library.

ISBN: HB: 978-0-85785-232-8
PB: 978-0-85785-233-5
ePDF: 978-1-47258-841-8
ePub: 978-0-85785-234-2

Library of Congress Cataloging-in-Publication Data
A catalog record for this book is available from the Library of Congress.

Typeset by Fakenham Prepress Solutions, Fakenham, Norfolk, NR21 8NN
Printed and bound in India

"She feels guilty if she doesn't buy it, she feels guilty if she buys and doesn't eat it, she feels guilty when she sees it in the fridge, she feels guilty when she throws it away."
(Don DeLillo, *White Noise*, 1985)

Contents

Acknowledgments

The research that informs this book was made possible through a Post-Doctoral Research Fellowship at the University of Manchester's Sustainable Consumption Institute, and more recently by funding from the Economic and Social Research Council (ES/L00514X/1). Additional writing was undertaken as a visiting researcher on the Economic and Social Research Council funded "Waste of the World" programme (RES000232007).

I am grateful to my friends and colleagues in the Sustainable Consumption Institute for creating the intellectual culture that has given rise to some of the ideas in the pages that follow. In particular I would like to thank Dale Southerton, Alan Warde, Daniel Welch, Luke Yates, Alison Browne, Andrew McMeekin, Sally Gee, and Elvira Uyarra. Additionally I would like to thank my friends and colleagues in the Sociology department at the University of Manchester, including Elisa Bellotti, Wendy Bottero, Nick Crossley, Anna Einarsdottir, Brian Heaphy, and Joseph Ibrahim for various forms of advice, support and encouragement. Particular thanks are due to my good friend and office mate James Rhodes.

For many thought-provoking discussions of food, food waste and related intellectual themes I would like to thank Hugh Campbell, Nicky Gregson, Peter Jackson, Alan Metcalfe, Matt Watson, Angela Meah, Justin Spinney, Monica Truninger, and Ben Coles. Particular thanks are due to Anne Murcott. I shall refrain from embarrassing her by pointing out that it would not be possible for a British sociologist to write a book such as this were it not for the ground that she broke, and instead express my gratitude for her generosity, guidance, and friendship. I am especially grateful to her for indulging my decision to stop writing this book, and then leaving it a month or so before somehow cajoling me (with a little help from Hugh Campbell) into resuming work on it.

This book has been a long time in the making and various parts of it have been tried out at a number of different conferences over the last three years. The ideas have certainly been sharpened by useful feedback and comments from colleagues too numerous to mention. In particular, my participation in the FOODSCAPES conference (organized by the University of Graz, Austria) in September 2013 gave me a unique opportunity to try the book out "as a whole" at a crucial juncture. I am sincerely grateful to everybody who took the time to offer useful thoughts and criticisms, especially Mike Goodman, Mara Miele, Julie Guthman, and Melissa Caldwell. Additionally, I have been fortunate enough to interact with a number of people who are involved in very practical efforts to research and reduce food waste. I cannot overstate how valuable this has been and in particular, I would like to thank Tom Quested for his continued engagement and insightful conversations.

Back in the real world I would very much like to thank my parents Mike and Jeannette, and my sister Joanne. I thank them for many things but mainly I hope that this book makes up for some of my own adolescent moralizing about food. Thanks also to two of my oldest friends: Nick Wilshin and Nick Jenkins, and to Kimberley de Jong (who also deserves thanks for her help with the figures in Chapter 8). Much of this book was written on Fridays in the spring and summer of 2013 and I am thankful to the various combinations of people with whom I spent Thursday evenings drinking rum, including Sarah Owen, Nick Clough, Benn Smith, and Jeremy Lane. Particular thanks must go to Mike Hewitson and Catherine Metzger—both for being there (almost) every Thursday, and for consistently providing terrific company.

Bringing things back to the book, I thank Daniel Miller for supporting the proposal and to everybody at Berg/Bloomsbury for providing such excellent support at every step of the way. Particular thanks are due to Louise Butler—not least for her endless patience. I am grateful to Daniel Miller, Zsuzsa Gille, Nicky Gregson, Anne Murcott and in particular—Melissa Caldwell for their comments on the original proposal and/or the final manuscript. Their comments and suggestions have no doubt strengthened the quality of the finished product but, of course, the usual disclaimers apply.

Finally, and above all, I am indebted to those who accommodated my sustained presence in their homes during the course of the fieldwork on which this book is based.

David Evans
Salford
January 2014

Prologue: The Social Life (and Death) of Food

This book is concerned with how and why households end up wasting food that they have purchased for consumption. As such, its premise is relatively straightforward: to explore how stuff that is understood as "food" eventually becomes "waste." I am going to begin with a story about broccoli and this story begins in the supermarket. However unlike Fischer and Benson, whose excellent study (2006) traces broccoli back from the supermarket to the Mayan farmers in highland Guatemala who produced it, and in doing so offers a powerful analysis of globalization, desire and political economic relations of power; I am going to take an altogether more familiar journey. My story simply follows the broccoli back from the supermarket, into somebody's home and eventually their bin.

BROCCOLI

And so this story begins in the supermarket, where Sadie has graciously allowed me to join her as she goes about the task of doing her grocery shopping. Sadie is in her early forties and lives with her husband and two young children. Both she and her husband are busy, professional workers who tend to share responsibility for cooking, however Sadie is responsible for the vast majority of food shopping. As we walk around the fruit and vegetable aisles in the supermarket, she picks up a broccoli head and explains to me that this is an item of food that gets wasted a lot in their household as it is rare for them to eat all that they buy. When she has finished explaining this to me, she places the broccoli in her shopping trolley. It is curious that as somebody who is in fact deeply troubled by the act of wasting this—or indeed any—food, she continues to purchase it when it is likely that she will end up placing it in the bin. I point this out to her and it leads to a discussion about the importance of buying broccoli on the grounds that it is healthy and "one of those things that you are *supposed* to eat." Still standing in the vegetable aisle, Sadie picks the broccoli out of the trolley and elaborates that by looking at it, you can tell that it is fresh, wholesome and good for you. Actually, it transpires, it is not just her health that she is thinking about here—it is the health of her husband and children. It goes back in the trolley and we carry on shopping.

Three days later, I am in Sadie's kitchen where she has invited me to accompany and observe her as she prepares an evening meal for her family. Roughly half of the broccoli florets are getting steamed along with some carrots and cauliflower, forming an accompaniment to some new potatoes and salmon baked with lemon juice, parsley and a small amount of garlic. It smells really good. The remainder of the broccoli florets—along with about the same amount of cauliflower and what is left of the bag of carrots—gets wrapped up and placed back in the fridge. Incidentally, although edible, the stalk of the broccoli is not something that Sadie (in common with much of the U.K. population) considers as "food" and so it does not register as, or feature in, her understandings of food waste. The following week I am once again in Sadie's kitchen following a trip to the supermarket, and she is putting away the shopping that she has just acquired. As part of this process she needs to make some room in the fridge. This involves re-organizing some of the items that are in there, but it also involves throwing things out. Of interest here is that the leftover broccoli remains uneaten and by now, it does not look quite so fresh, enticing and wholesome. In fact it looks rather limp, feels a bit soft and appears to have suffered a degree of discoloration. As a result, it becomes a casualty of this "sorting out" process and ends up in the bin, which—as will be seen—means that it will most likely be carried off into the waste stream.

So items that were once understood as food have now been configured as waste, and effectively this happened when a newer, fresher, counterpart was acquired. You might be thinking "well why purchase new broccoli in the first place?" however the analysis that follows suggests that there are many reasons for doing so and that, certainly, the activity of "feeding the family" (DeVault 1991) is so heavily routinized and entwined with a number of other pressures that conscious and "rational" deliberation rarely enters into it. For now, it is worth acknowledging that there are clearly processes of physical decay at work here. As a book in the *Materializing Culture* series, it will not surprise you to see a discussion of the social life of things (Appadurai 1986). However it is important to signal that things also have a physical life that unravels and intersects with the trajectories of their social life, and for the purposes of this book—their death. In all likelihood the broccoli was probably destined not to be eaten at the point that it went back in the fridge, long before its eventual fate was acknowledged. However in keeping it around for a while, processes of physical decay conspire to position the old broccoli as unsuitable for ingestion, or at least *less* suitable than the new arrival. In turn, this helps to legitimize its consignment to the category of "waste" and the act of binning it. True enough, it did not reach the point at which it was unsafe to eat but to salvage it would have risked the future of the "good" broccoli that had just been purchased.

Of course, it *could* have been eaten at some point in between placing it in the fridge and eventually placing it in the bin. However, again, there are many valid and understandable reasons why this did not happen. For example, Sadie's children will only eat broccoli in combination with baked salmon and she does not wish to cook this more than once a week in case they get bored of it and then refuse to eat broccoli at all. Additionally, Sadie would happily buy the broccoli in a smaller quantity; however, she does not have the option of doing so because the supermarket only sells whole broccoli heads. You might be thinking that perhaps she does not need to buy broccoli *and* carrots *and* cauliflower, and that it would be better just to buy one item and waste none of it. Or perhaps you might be thinking that it would make more sense for her to purchase frozen vegetables that are less susceptible to rapid decay. Fine. However, convention dictates that Sadie should cook and eat "properly", and this is commonly understood as a matter of cooking and eating a *variety* of *fresh* ingredients. I highlight this to signal some of the processes through which food becomes waste and that they are not as simple as people making irresponsible choices because they do not care about the consequences of doing so. In fact, I am trying to suggest (and will go on to argue) that the reasons for food going to waste are rarely reducible to the households—less still the individuals—who end up carrying out the act of binning.

RUBICON

The second story is about a carton of Rubicon (a range of tropical fruit drinks sold in the U.K.) lychee and again, it starts in the supermarket. This time, however, I follow its passage through my own home and eventually, down the drain. I must confess to being slightly reticent about writing myself into this prologue and taking up space that could have been used to present another ethnographic encounter. Empirical material is almost certainly preferable to self-reflection but as social scientists, it is also important to guard against the tendency to view ourselves as outside of, or external to, the phenomena that we observe, describe and theorize. This is especially true to ethnographers, particular those who do research "at home," in the home, and on morally loaded issues such as food waste. My logic in giving an anecdote from my own life is by way of acknowledgment that I am not immune to the processes and practices that are discussed in the pages that follow.

I did not buy this bottle of Rubicon for the laudable reasons—as was the case with Sadie's broccoli—of looking after myself or ensuring that my loved ones eat and drink properly. I bought it by mistake. I actually intended to buy the sparkling mango Rubicon that I remembered trying a few weeks earlier as an accompaniment to my lunch in one of Manchester's 'rice and three' eateries (if you get a chance to go to one, you should go). However, despite spending a good deal of time hanging around in supermarkets doing fieldwork; when it comes to doing my own shopping, I get in and I get out as quickly as is humanly possible. On this occasion, my proclivity for rushing led to me putting the flat (not sparkling), carton (not can) of lychee (not mango) Rubicon into my trolley. Several days later when I sat down to drink it, I was disappointed to realize that I had picked up the wrong drink, and that I really did not like the item that I had purchased. I tried to give it away to several friends and colleagues. However, as will be seen later, it is often very difficult to gift or re-circulate food and drink in a contemporary U.K. context. My solution was to put it in my fridge where I could just forget about it and get on with my life. As I did this, I told myself that I would make a fruit punch with it when the sun came out but I never did. In any case, I couldn't *really* forget about it and it continued to trouble me, knowing it was there but knowing that I could not find a use for it. And so when I reached the point in the year at which I decide to "use up" the things that I have in my fridge and freezer; I poured this down the drain (it was perfectly fit for human consumption) and assuaged my guilt by noting that I had at least recycled the bottle, made some effort to find a use for it and kept it around for a respectable period of time.

So there you have it: I waste food and like most people, I don't feel particularly good about it. My point in stating the obvious is to clarify upfront that I am not looking to pass judgment on or to criticize the persons and practices discussed in the chapters that follow. To the contrary, this book is intended as a rejoinder to the alarmist and moralistic tendency to observe current levels of waste generation and then read back from these to make unsubstantiated inferences about what goes on in people's homes and the reasons why they waste food. I do not dispute that current volumes of household food waste are problematic in a number of registers—after all, it wasn't just intellectual curiosity that led me to this area of research. However, I do not accept explanations (worse still, assumptions) that reduce the problem to a matter of individual consumer behavior and/or an anomalously profligate culture that is ignorant to the source, value, and ways of correctly using food. Accordingly the thrust of the argument developed here is that the passage of "food" into "waste" occurs as a more or less mundane consequence of the ways in which practices of everyday and domestic life are currently carried out, and the various factors that shape the prevailing organization of food consumption.

But we are getting ahead of ourselves now insofar as there is a bit of work to be done before I can make this argument or give academic substance to the stories that I just told. And so please turn the page and begin at the beginning.

–1–

Bringing Waste to The Table

Having opened with some grounded and situated stories, this chapter takes a step back to scale the heights of the broader academic debates and emerging political concerns that provide the impetus for writing (and reading) a book about food waste. I begin by discussing recent trends across the social sciences, and in cultural theory, that have begun to position "waste" as intellectually interesting before drawing attention to the neglect of food in the midst of these developments. Accordingly I make a case for paying social scientific attention to food waste, both in terms of contributing to the development of waste scholarship and engaging with an issue that is of increasing importance in the realms of policy and regulation, cultural politics, and environmental debate. With that in place, I map out how the book will proceed and the approach to food waste that will be taken here.

WASTE MATTERS

It is perhaps a little peculiar to start with the assertion that waste could in any way matter and it is perhaps more peculiar still to suggest that it could be of intellectual or analytic significance. Traditionally waste has been approached in very particular ways, giving rise to an academic division of labor in which it has long been invisible to the gaze of the social sciences. To understand this, it is important to summarize the (implicit) assumptions that have conventionally been made about waste. They are as follows: (1) that it is a fixed and self-evident category—an innate characteristic of certain things or things in a certain state; (2) that things categorized as waste are either worthless or harmful, and so in need of being separated and distanced from the societies that produced them; (3) that this separation and distancing is a task for waste management and simultaneously, that things are categorized as waste on the basis of their need to be managed (Gregson and Crang 2010); and (4) that waste is located at the end-of-pipe and so is uncomplicatedly viewed as that which is leftover, the redundant and final by-products of cultural and economic organization. Taken together, these tendencies have positioned waste as a void that lies beyond the boundaries of the social and as such, the mere shadow of processes that social scientists are interested in. So where social scientists have enthusiastically explored the production, distribution, purchase and use of things, waste has remained an afterthought, the mere afterwards of these activities, and of interest only to certain branches of the social sciences such as environmental policy and planning. This has no doubt given rise to interesting researches around the themes of governance, waste policy, and waste management (for example Davoudi 2000; Petts 2004; Chilvers and Burgess 2008), however these topics are rather niche, and tangential to mainstream social science priorities.

Of course waste can be—and has been—imagined in different ways. As Gay Hawkins points out, when waste "is used in a normative sense, as a category of judgment, meanings proliferate fast" (2006: vii). However, these perspectives have not necessarily led to serious or sustained engagement with waste, nor is their relevance to broader social scientific endeavor immediately apparent. For a start, there are approaches that conceptualize waste as hazardous or contaminating, leading to researches on risks and perceptions of risks, as well as more sociological efforts to extend Beck's (1992) risk society thesis to analyses of waste (Van Loon 2002; cf. Gille 2013). Work in the tradition of environmental justice has demonstrated how social and spatial inequalities—typically along the lines of race and class—are marked and mirrored by exposure or proximity to waste (Bullard 1983; Heiman 1996; Martuzzi et al. 2010; Meagher 2010). More generally, various social histories (Laporte 1999; Melosi 2004) have demonstrated how (civilizing) processes of social organization and modernization rest on concomitant efforts to expel, distance, and hide wastes from the societies that produced them. Again, this is interesting stuff but these analyses continue to locate waste beyond the boundaries of the social and position it as something negative or a problem to be managed.

There is also a tendency to deploy waste as a metaphorical device and amongst other things, it has served rather well as a shorthand for the unproductive expenditure of time and money (Schor 1998), the alleged excesses of global consumer capitalism (Packard 1961) and environmental destruction (Redclift 1996). Allied to this, one might even suggest that—in actuality—the social sciences have long been pre-occupied with residual categories. As Munro (2013) describes:

> This is not just to note classics of sociology, such as *Street Corner Society* (Whyte 1943) and *The Police on Skid Row* (Bittner 1967), engage [...] It is to identify how modern programmes like medicine harbour designs that inevitably proceed

by throwing out the chronically ill as 'crocks' (Becker 1993), the homeless as 'normal rubbish' (Jeffery 1979), and the frail as 'bedblockers' (Latimer 2000). So too Bauman (2004) lays what he calls 'wasted lives' firmly at the door of modernity, suggesting presciently that in the future the 'outcasts' of globalization will have nowhere to go. (Munro 2013: 221)

This signals some of the ways in which waste might be of more obvious relevance to mainstream social science research, however, work in this spirit does not place waste at the center of its analysis (although see Scanlan 2005), nor does it engage with the material reality of waste matter. Instead, waste remains an allegory that can only be used to gesture back and reveal something about the societies and systems that produced and rejected it.

In this book, I put forward an account that suspends judgment to recognize that the definition of food waste is not fixed, and that it is not an unambiguously negative phenomenon. However, I also wish to acknowledge the "concrete and socially consequential materiality" (Gille 2010: 1056) of food waste and so this requires a focus on the relationships (cultural, economic, technological, political and social) in which it is embedded alongside the various ways in which it is categorized, placed, represented, and managed. I do not conceptualize food waste as the end point in linear processes of production, consumption, and disposal insofar as waste can arise at multiple sites within the food chain, and with tangible consequences for the economic and cultural organization of food systems. Allied to this, I argue that food waste provides the generative and constitutive basis (not the mere afterwards) for the practices that shape the organization of everyday life. In order to take this position, inspiration is drawn from recent developments that place waste at the center of social scientific analyses to explore its dynamic and shifting role in the process of social organization without denying its concrete materiality. I am thinking specifically of work by Zsuzsa Gille, Nicky Gregson, Gay Hawkins and Martin O'Brien. However, before discussing these in more detail, interested readers may welcome some consideration of the intellectual precursors to these ideas.[1]

To begin, there are threads of work that systematically attend to residual phenomena and so acknowledge their role in processes of social organization and social change. For example, Mary Douglas' *Purity and Danger* (1966) drew attention to the cultural categorization of dirt and the analytic importance of investigating the classificatory systems that produce and reject this so-called "matter out of place." Later, Michael Thompson's quietly influential *Rubbish Theory* (1979) suggested that the process of categorizing rubbish is one part of a wider system of categorization and valuation. For Thompson, rubbish is not waste in the sense of being redundant and worthless stuff, rather it is a "region of flexibility" that resides between transient (decreasing) value and durable (increasing, or at least stable) value. Essentially, he makes the case that waste may or may not facilitate movements between transient and durable value, and is therefore central to understandings of how value is socially controlled. The decisive formulation, however, came with John Scanlan's *On Garbage* (2005) that explores the connections between "the variety of hidden, forgotten, thrown away and residual phenomena that attend life at all times" (2005: 8). In doing so, he eloquently demonstrates that metaphorical garbage—the detached leftovers of separating the valuable from the worthless—is at once omnipresent and central to (Western) ways of thinking about the world. In recognizing the constitutive role of residual categories, this work places them at the center of social scientific endeavor. It also recognizes "waste" as a category that is inherently malleable as well as the complexity of meanings attributed to it. However, again, these approaches do not sufficiently acknowledge the concrete and consequential materiality of waste matter.

From a slightly different angle, there are lines of thinking that place waste—in all its brute physical glory—at the center of their analysis and use it as a route into theorizing broader cultural and economic processes. For example, Susan Strasser's *Waste Not Want Not* (1999) uses changing notions of trash in order to trace a social history of production, consumption, and use. Famously, William Rathje began his work on what he called "garbology" in the early 1970s (collaborating later with Cullen Murphy [1992]) in which they applied archeological methods to the study of garbage, with the suggestion that explorations of trash yield important insights into the cultures that produce it. Central to this endeavor is the idea that waste cannot be studied "in the abstract" and that garbology requires physical contact with "hundreds of tons" of waste material (Rathje and Murphy 1992: 9). More generally a good deal of archeological and anthropological work has signaled the importance of studying discarded materials. For example Gavin Lucas' early plea (2002) for material culture scholarship to pay attention to waste suggested that disposability and the removal of things from domestic economies might be a useful starting point for doing so. Similarly, Laurence Douny's study amongst the Dogon of Mali (2007) focusses on the materiality of domestic waste to reveal the more positive connotations attached to things—animal excrement, bodily dirt, litter, and unwashed cooking utensils—that Western cosmologies would categorize as worthless or unclean. Further, she suggests that Western conceptions of waste—as useless and redundant—tend only to apply to "elements that stand outside domestic life" (2007: 313) in the Dogon. This work directly confronts the materiality of waste whilst also acknowledging that it is not a fixed category. Further, in a debt to Mary Douglas, it demonstrates how waste materializes otherwise intangible processes of cultural categorization. What is missing, I think, is recognition that quite aside from simply revealing who we are; our trash and garbage is constitutive of how we live in the world.

Returning now to the new directions in waste scholarship that appear to synthesize some of these ideas. Firstly, Gay Hawkins' *The Ethics of Waste: How we Relate to Rubbish* (2006) represents an important challenge to existing understandings of our relationships to waste, which had hitherto been dominated by environmental discourse and alarmist rhetoric. She argues that "disenchantment stories" and narratives of "paradise lost" have worked to position waste as emblematic of humankind's alienation from, and consequent disregard for, the natural world—bringing about a politics based on the imperative to reform the self in the name of nature. Against this, she suggests that waste and not the environment should be placed at the center of analysis. In foregrounding waste, her approach is one of encountering its empirical—and material—reality and considering how it shapes the processes and habits through which we consume, value, classify, and manage things. So for example she demonstrates that our responses to human excrement are constitutive of the relationship between the public and the private, and generative of certain routines of self-maintenance and embodiment.

Meanwhile Martin O'Brien's *A Crisis of Waste* (2007) suggests that the invisibility of waste in sociological thought is a reflection of its invisibility in popular and political imaginations, and so he sets out to rescue it, give it the scholarly attention that it deserves and develop a "rubbish imagination" that takes seriously the generative role of waste in social life. He urges that contemporary Western societies should be understood as "rubbish societies"—not in the sense that they are "throwaway cultures" but, rather, that rubbish is and always has been central to processes of social organization. He suggests that sociology might usefully focus on the practices, institutions, innovations and relations that have emerged to govern waste and its transformation into value. Within sociology, as well, Zsuzsa Gille's *From the Cult of Waste to the Trash Heap of History* (2007) makes clear that waste is neither a fixed category nor the simple outcome of policies that define things as such. Rather she develops the concept of "waste regimes" to account for the institutions and conventions that determine what wastes are considered valuable and the ways in which their production and distribution is managed, represented and politicized. She highlights how these regimes vary across space and time and so highlights the contingent and relational character of "waste" whilst continuing to take seriously the physical reality of these materials. Crucially, in addition to acknowledging that differing definitions of waste are expressive of different regimes; she highlights that they are constitutive and sustaining of them.

Finally, there is work that comes ostensibly out of material culture scholarship to arrive at a similar, or at least related, set of insights. Notably, this is the work of Nicky Gregson who has—across a number of projects and with a range of collaborators—explored human relationships with waste at a variety of scales whilst attending to a number of theoretical and substantive concerns. Her earlier work on second-hand consumption (Gregson and Crewe 2003) led to a concern with how and why things pass into economies of re-use. Accordingly, her ethnographic work on the divestment and disposal of ordinary consumer objects (Gregson 2007; Gregson et al. 2007a, 2007b) shows how sacrifice and the process of ridding is generative of—amongst other things—personhood, self-renewal, and networks of relationships between person and things (see also Lucy Norris' work [2004] on the disposal of clothing in India). This in turn led to work that looked beyond the household to recognize that waste is not simply an end-of-pipe issue. Here, she has explored the global flows of materials as things fall apart or are purposely disassembled as well as highlighting the various economies that are created and sustained by these processes (Gregson, Crang et al. 2010). Additionally, she has illustrated how the work of demolition unearths materials in transformative states—notably asbestos (Gregson, Watkins et al. 2010)—that play a vital and performative role in configuring the economies and economics of disposal.

It is instructive, albeit curious, to note that despite the vitality of contemporary waste scholarship, relatively little attention has been paid to food. Social scientists working with these perspectives have not—until very recently—paid attention directly or specifically to food waste. There have been passing references in sociological and anthropological analyses of food (for example Goody 1982; Fine 1996), theoretical consideration of the ways in which the availability of conduits for disposal govern what we eat (Munro, 1995) and more recently, work that extends (following Hetherington, 2004 and the work of Nicky Gregson) work on material culture and consumption as disposal to analyses of food waste (Cappellini 2009; Evans 2011a, 2012a, 2012b). In 2013 *Waste Matters: New Perspectives on Food and Society* (Evans et al. 2013b) was published, and this edited collection sought—very consciously—to extend recent developments in waste scholarship to engage more thoroughly with food waste. Effectively, it starts to populate the sketch of potential approaches to food waste offered by Catherine Alexander and her colleagues (Alexander et al. 2013) and as such, includes contributions that consider food waste in relation to questions of political economy (Gille 2013; Krzywoszynska 2013; O'Brien, 2013); the cultures, ideologies and politics of food and consumption (Cappellini and Parsons 2013; Meah 2013: Metcalfe et al. 2013; Watson) and, post-humanist perspectives (Milne 2013; Hawkins 2013). In doing so, it demonstrates the importance of analyzing waste in terms of developing understandings of food (Coles and Hallet 2013; Edwards and Mercer 2013) and social theory more generally (Munro 2013). Despite this publication, food waste remains an under-researched and under-theorized topic, and in-depth, empirically grounded accounts are thin on the ground. The short book in your hands aims to provide a systematic and focussed analysis of household food waste. However before saying more about this book, it is worth considering in more detail the non-academic concerns that have emerged around the origins and consequences of food waste.

THE FOOD THAT WE WASTE

The aforementioned dearth of social science engagement with food waste is perhaps surprising given the prevalence of these concerns in food policy, cultural politics, and environmental debate. As will be seen, this book offers a social scientific and as far as is possible—detached yet empathetic account of some of the processes that lie behind the generation of household food waste. As such, it is not intended as an activist or campaigning book that seeks to expose and quantify current volumes of waste generation (see Stuart 2009; Bloom 2010 for excellent examples of this genre). That said, nothing in these pages is intended to de-problematize food waste as a social and ethical issue. As such, it is worth jumping from the heights of academic debate to the equally lofty territory where food waste is coming to matter as a political priority.

A recent report by the Food and Agriculture Organization of the United Nations (FAO 2011) estimates that globally, one third of the food produced for consumption is wasted—or otherwise lost—each year. This amounts to 1.3 billion tons annually and these losses and wastes occur throughout the food chain in agricultural production, processing, distribution, retail, and final consumption. Hot on the heels of this publication, the Institution of Mechanical Engineers delivered a report entitled *Global Food Waste Not, Want Not* (IMechE 2013) in which they estimate that up to 50 percent of all food produced never reaches a human stomach. Figures such as these are no doubt startling in their own right but it is also worth pausing to consider why they should give such cause for alarm. For a start, it is estimated that there are 870 million under-nourished people in the world (FAO, 2012) and there is an undeniable perversity in food going to waste whilst this many people go hungry. Of course it would be overly simplistic to suggest that wasted food could be used to feed the hungry but the connections between food abundance, food waste, and food poverty are nevertheless "real" (Stuart 2009: xvi). Digging a little deeper, it is equally perverse that finite resources (land, water, energy) are currently being used to produce food that goes uneaten, and that it would undoubtedly be more just and efficient if they were to be allocated to the production of food that saves others from starvation. This connects to the more general issue of food security insofar as there are very real demands for global food production to increase in order to meet the needs of a growing—and increasingly affluent—world population. The challenge of producing sufficient safe and nutritious food is not trivial and it is perfectly logical to insist (Stuart 2009; FAO 2011) that reducing food waste should be a priority in terms of increasing the efficiency of food chains and reducing some of the pressure on finite resources.

Allied to concerns about food security are the environmental impacts of global food production and food waste. As it stands, the demands made on finite resources to meet current levels of food production are environmentally damaging. As land is turned over to agricultural purposes, existing eco-systems are destroyed. In addition to the loss of biodiversity, deforestation entails the release of CO_2 and other greenhouse gases into the atmosphere. These emissions are tied intimately to anthropogenic climate change and disruptions to hydrological cycles and soil quality, to the point that land given over to agriculture may not—ironically enough—be productive for these purposes in the longer term. Again, the argument runs that this level of environmental degradation is not necessary to grow enough food to feed the world's population, and as Tristram Stuart (2009) so eloquently advocates: reducing waste is a powerful way of relieving some of the pressure on the world's remaining eco-systems and changing climate. Add to that the fact that wasted food carries additional environmental burdens in terms of unnecessary CO_2 emissions embedded in its production and the release of harmful greenhouse gases (especially methane) as it rots in landfill, and the environmental imperative to tackle the issue becomes clear. Taking the environmental consequences of wasted food and putting them alongside the social implications detailed above—not to mention the obvious losses of economic value that it entails—it becomes clear why many people talk and think in terms of a global food waste scandal. Even for those who resist the language of panic and crisis, there is no denying that it is something that is worth thinking about and tackling.

In recent years, the issue of food waste has become an increasing concern for governments and their populations. A discussion of the precise contours of the contemporary debate and its genesis is beyond the scope of this short introduction (although see Evans et al. 2013a for fuller discussion), but it is instructive to note that the very fact that the FAO has looked into the problem signals it is an issue of global political significance, just as the success and profile of activists like Stuart and Bloom provide a testimony to its relevance in public imaginations. Additionally, it is worth noting that it is taking center stage in the European Union (E.U.) and that on January 19, 2012, the European Parliament called on the European Commission (E.C.) to halve current volumes of food waste (E.C. estimates suggest 90 million tons are produced annually in the E.U.) by 2025. There was even talk of imagining 2014 as the "European year against food waste." The E.U. is not alone in making food waste a priority and as figures emerge about the extent of food waste in America, Australia, China, The Netherlands and so on, so too does the imperative to do something about it. It should be noted that food waste is also a problem in less developed countries and here, the issue is framed as one of food "loss" (FAO 2011) arising post-harvest due to insufficient technology and planning. These losses escape the moral opprobrium directed at post-consumer "waste" in developed nations and so are seen as less of a consumption-related problem. Without disputing that losses throughout the food chain are interesting and worthy of in-depth study, this book is focussed on the wastes identified and attributed to actors at the end of the chain.

Specifically, this is a book about food waste in U.K. households, since this is where the empirical material that informs the analysis is drawn. It is not difficult to produce startling statistics or analyses that locate households and consumers (in the affluent world) at the heart of the global food crisis. For example, influential work by the U.K.'s Waste and Resources Action Programme (WRAP)—a not for profit company set up in 2000 in response to the demands of the E.U.'s 1999 landfill directive and supported by funding from the four national governments of the U.K.—has quantified the amount of food and drink wasted by households and contextualized the extent of the problem. By their estimates (WRAP 2011; see also Quested et al. 2013) U.K. households wasted 7.2 million tons of food and drink in 2010 and 4.4 million tons could have been avoided. Again, the environmental and social impacts are significant. For example, the greenhouse gas emissions associated with avoidable food waste are equivalent to 17 million tons of CO_2—roughly the same amount that is generated by a quarter of the cars in use on U.K.

roads. Similarly it is instructive to note the perversity of food waste and food poverty co-existing, even within the U.K., as an ever-increasing number of people are at risk of not having sufficient access to food. For example the Trusell Trust—a charitable organization that runs the U.K.'s largest network of food banks—reports doubling the number of food parcels that it issued between 2011 and 2012. In addition to the social and environmental implications associated with household food waste in the U.K., there are obvious economic losses. WRAP's estimates suggest £12 billion annually—equivalent to £480 per household.

With similar figures and issues being reported in relation to other nation states and the Institution of Mechanical Engineers' report suggesting that 30–50 percent of food purchased in developed nations is thrown away "by the purchaser," it is perhaps not surprising that aggregate estimates suggest that over 40 percent of food waste in industrialized countries occurs towards the end of the food chain—at the levels of retail and final consumption (FAO 2011). There is no doubt that in popular and political imaginations, food waste is positioned as an "end of pipe" problem with the emphasis for responding to it placed on households, consumers, and public systems of waste management (Alexander et al. 2013). As will become clear, this framing is problematic but for now the point remains that households—especially those in the global North—are currently implicated in the global food waste scandal and yet very little is known about household practices of food waste generation. As Bulkeley and Gregson (2009) point out, there is something of a divide between waste policy and research on the one hand, and those branches of academia that deal with the household dynamics and processes of consumption on the other. This situation is, I would argue, untenable since if there is to be any hope of reducing waste in households; there is a need for much closer engagement with what actually goes on "behind closed doors" (Miller 2001a), and to understand why people actually waste food in the first place. Rectifying this lacuna provided the major impetus for carrying out the empirical work that informs the analysis that follows and indeed, for writing this book.

THE BOOK

This is not a book about the global food waste scandal (Tristram Stuart and Jonathan Bloom do a far better job than I ever could), nor is it a book about the volume of food that is wasted by U.K. households (WRAP's estimates and associated papers by Tom Quested and colleagues are far better placed).

This is a book about the processes through which stuff that is "food" becomes stuff that is "waste," and so it descends from the heights of trends in waste scholarship and concerns about the global food waste crisis to get down and dirty. It draws specifically on empirical material derived from an ethnographic study of household food waste in the North West of the United Kingdom and whilst it necessarily keeps an eye on these bigger issues, the focus is on giving an account of the material gathered during the fieldwork. In doing so, this book attempts to bring together three key themes: (1) the dynamics of everyday life and the ways in which waste is embedded in these flows and practices; (2) the home as research context (Pink 2004), the primary locus of consumption (Miller 2001a) and the site at which efforts to reduce food waste are currently focussed; and (3) food as a specific genre of material culture.

These concerns run throughout the chapters that follow as I explore how and why food that is purchased for consumption comes to be wasted by households. In Chapter 2, I set out the theoretical and methodological approach that informs the analysis. Chapters 3 and 4 are intended as a pair of substantive sections that begin to map the passage of "food" into "waste" by exploring the various reasons why households end up with more food than is required for their perceived and immediate requirements of consumption. Chapter 5 takes these "surplus" foodstuffs and provides the theoretical resources to make sense of them whilst shedding empirical light on the moments when their future is yet to be decided. Chapters 6 and 7 are intended as another companion pair, given this time to an exploration of how surplus foodstuffs become "excess" alongside the movements, placings and practices that work to configure them as waste. To conclude, in Chapter 8, I bring these insights together to sketch out a sociological theory of household food waste and offer a series of practical reflections on the implications of the approach taken here for real-world initiatives to reduce current volumes of household food waste.

This book is intended partly as a monograph—written as an ethnography of food waste in some U.K. households—and partly as a resource for students insofar as it covers a number of concepts that help to engage academically with the issue. Additionally, it is hoped that it will be of relevance to those with an interest in food and/or waste, just as the approach taken here is intended to provide material for colleagues whose work—as my subtitle suggests—looks at home consumption, material culture and everyday life.

Ordinary Domestic Practice: Conceptualizing, Researching, Representing

In public and policy debates about food waste, households and consumers are positioned and represented in very particular ways. At worst, they are blamed and chastised for current levels of waste generation and at best, responsibilities for affecting change are located at their door. In this chapter, I begin by considering these tendencies and suggesting that this is neither an adequate nor accurate picture of why households waste food. The prologue gave a flavor and indication of the ways in which food waste can be interpreted as the fallout of day-to-day life and Chapter 1 signaled the importance of understanding what goes on "behind closed doors" if there is to be any possibility of reducing the volume of food that is currently wasted at the level of the household. I now set out the academic debates that led my own analysis of consumption and waste into people's homes and everyday lives. With this in place, I give details of the ethnographic study that informs my analysis alongside reflection on how these data will be utilized in the remainder of the book.

HOUSEHOLDS, CONSUMERS, AND THE GLOBAL FOOD WASTE SCANDAL

In the previous chapter, I illustrated how food waste is currently imagined as an "end of pipe" problem in which households and consumers are positioned as the main offenders. In doing so, I presented some of the well-known statistics that have been deployed in support of this. Taking a more qualitative look at the content of debates about food waste in the realms of formal and cultural politics, it becomes even clearer that households and consumers are firmly on the agenda when it comes to framing the problem and thinking about possible solutions. For example, the aforementioned Institution of Mechanical Engineers report chastises "the most 'advanced' and affluent societies where the largest quantities of food are wasted at the consumer end of the chain" (2013: 22), citing excessive purchasing, the demand for aesthetic perfection, poor understandings of "use by" labeling and the under-valuing of food by households as the main explanations for this. Further, they invoke the familiar refrain that contemporary households are "merely food consumers" who belong to a "culture with little understanding of the source and value of food" (2013: 27). They are by no means alone in framing the issue in this way. For example the Food and Agricultural Organization (FAO) of the United Nations is quite explicit that affluence, consumer attitudes and a lack of awareness are to blame (FAO 2011: 14) just as the European Commission offers "lack of awareness, lack of shopping planning, confusion about 'best before' and 'use by' date labels, lack of knowledge on how to cook with leftovers (households)" at the top of its list of reasons for food waste generation.[1]

Many commentators do not go so far down the route of blaming the consumer (Evans 2011a), however even here, the recommendations on how to reduce food waste seem to only target the knowledge and attitudes of individuals in an attempt to affect the choices that they make and the behaviors that they undertake. For example, Stuart (2009: 77) suggests a strategy of raising awareness of the "non-financial costs of wasting food" (environmental impacts, world hunger) just as WRAP's *lovefoodhatewaste* campaign[2] provides information intended to enable individuals who are already trying to behave differently. These suggestions are refreshingly well intentioned and non-judgmental, and they are most likely very effective, at least in some cases. However in positioning individual households and consumers as central to efforts to affect change, they reinforce the tendency to implicate them in the global food waste scandal. This is problematic insofar as it makes use of a very limited toolkit that elides a good deal of social science scholarship around household dynamics and processes of consumption. Allied to this, it means that existing initiatives are premised on inaccurate understandings of the reasons why households waste food in the first place, meaning that they may not bring about changes of the scale and type required. Before getting to this, it is important to reflect further on this tendency to individualize responsibilities for affecting change.

THE RESPONSIBILIZATION OF THE INDIVIDUAL CONSUMER

The location of households and consumers in public and policy debates about food waste is not surprising. In any number of debates relating to sustainability, climate change, public health and trade justice (to name just a few), consumers are positioned both as part of the problem and as part of the solution. In their analysis of ethical consumption, Clive Barnett and his colleagues (Barnett et al. 2011) offer a genealogical analysis of how "the consumer" has emerged as a subject position through which individuals are required to express their rights and responsibilities as citizens. Rallying against claims that consumption has recently and suddenly become ethically charged and politically loaded (see Micheletti's analysis of political consumerism 2003), they suggest that "the consumer" has been constituted and mobilized in various different ways throughout the course of history. In the case of ethical consumption—and they explicitly acknowledge that this extends to "recycling and waste campaigns" (Barnett et al. 2011: 15)—they suggest that this phenomenon needs to be understood in relation to the changing nature of political mobilization in which new *repertoires* (Norris 2007) of political action (e.g. boycotts and demonstrations) and new *agencies* for facilitating engagement (e.g. new social movements in the place of traditional party politics) can be identified. They attribute the growth of ethical consumption to "strategies and repertoires shared amongst a diverse range of governmental and non-governmental actors" (2011: 1) meaning that their analytic focus shifts away from the agency of individual ethical consumers, and towards the concerted efforts of organizations and institutions such as campaigns, lobby groups, and ethical trading associations.

In unpacking the ways in which notions of the individual consumer are worked up to the "surface of government" (the publically observable figure of ethical consumption campaigning), they suggest that activists and campaigners deploy "narrative resources of ethical responsibility" such that individuals experience the imperative to do something whilst feeling "empowered to act" and so taken together, are enroled in support of particular causes. They draw heavily on Foucault's theories of governmentality (see Dean 1999; Rose 1999) in order to consider the exercise of power in situations where notions of centralized, singular and sovereign rule make little sense. Governmentality theories address the emergence of a more subtle relationship between the ruler and the ruled by focussing on the co-evolution of the modern state and the idea of the autonomous individual. They highlight the ways in which contemporary forms of governing "the conduct of conduct" rest on the capacity for organization and self-government at levels below the state in order to achieve its objectives. Here power is not exercised in the denial of freedom and the policing of individuals; rather it is accomplished by creating—and working through—the capabilities of freely choosing subjects in order to achieve particular outcomes. Central to this endeavor is the autonomous individual's capacity for self-control and the existence of multiple authorities and agencies that can provide the expertise and knowledge required to ensure that people act as they are required to act. In the case of ethical consumption, Barnett et al. (2011) suggest that the phenomenon is best explained by the emergent requirement for "consumers" to work on themselves and transform their conduct with the help of a range of intermediaries. They cite Lockie's account of Australia's organic food sector (2002) as an example of analysis that demonstrates how retailers, nutritionists and market researchers work to circulate discourses of ethical responsibility and provide moral instruction to "consumers" (see also Littler 2009).

I am inclined to suggest that similar processes are currently at work in efforts to reduce household food waste. Discourses of responsibility are being actively produced and circulated by a range of governmental and non-governmental actors including international organizations (e.g. the FAO), formal political institutions (e.g. the European Commission), high-profile activists (e.g. Tristram Stuart), cultural figures (e.g. celebrity chefs), media outlets (including new social media), and even food retailers[3] (see Evans et al. 2013a). These intermediaries—as previously discussed—are framing food waste as a problem and possibility of consumer behavior.[4] It is possible to identify the use of calculative technologies such as figures that quantify the extent of the problem, demonstrate how much of it can be attributed to consumers and contextualize what this means "per household" (see Chapter 1). Efforts to use calculative technologies to make a collective of consumers knowledgable in public arenas can also be identified. For example, in early 2013 the Institution of Mechanical Engineers carried out a survey of U.K. "consumers" and discovered that 45 percent of people claim that the appearance of fruit and vegetables does not matter, and 10 percent claim that they actively seek imperfect items[5]. It will be recalled that consumer demand for aesthetic perfection is often cited as a reason for fruit and vegetables going to waste, and so these figures represent a useful resource for campaigners to put pressure on food businesses and policy makers.

In addition to mobilizing consumers and calling them to action, food waste campaigning involves efforts that empower consumers to act. These very often take the form of moral and practical instruction. For example, Jonathan Bloom's (2010) excellent exposé of waste in the American food system dedicates a chapter to household food waste ("Home is Where the Waste is") and in it, he follows a subtle and nuanced account of why people waste food with detailed advice—directed at households—on what can be done about it. He advises, among other things, that households should "plan meals," "make a list," "beware of bulk," "keep food visible," and "make friends with your freezer."

There is no doubt that Bloom's advice is well intentioned, thoughtful and likely to represent a useful set of tips for certain households in helping to deal with some of the food that they waste. I am certainly not seeking to dismiss or criticize it, nor am I trying to rehearse familiar critiques that link governmentality to the ills of neo-liberalism. Rather, my main concern with these moves to responsibilize the individual consumer—in common with Barnett et al. (2011)—is that they are based on the assumption that "consumer behavior" is something that can be rationally guided and that interventions will unproblematically produce the desired outcome. These assumptions gloss over the ways in which ordinary people go about doing consumption (and for that matter, ethics), and the ways in which it connects to the patterning and dynamics of everyday life. It is to these issues that I now turn.

CONSUMPTION AND THEORIES OF PRACTICE

In recent years, the sociology of consumption—at least in Northern Europe—has been heavily influenced by the so-called "practice turn" in social theory (Schatzki et al. 2001). This development has shifted the analytic focus of consumption scholarship away from "the consumer" and associated notions of individualism or sovereignty. Theories of practice encompass a diverse range of insights from social and cultural theory but they are held together by the ontological position that practices—as opposed to individuals, social structures or discourses—are the basic unit of social analysis. This invites a focus on the dynamics of the things that people do and at the most basic level, practices are best defined as routinized behaviors (Reckwitz 2002)—for example cooking, laundering, dwelling, cycling—that are undertaken without too much in the way of conscious deliberation on the part of the social actor. Each practice represents a co-ordinated nexus of doings and sayings (Schatzki 1996) and by this, it is meant that a practice encompasses both the practical activity and its representation. At any point in space and time, there exists an established set of understandings, procedures, and engagements that govern appropriate conduct within a particular practice (Warde 2005). In this view, individuals are not the autonomous architects of their own actions; they are carriers of practice—practitioners—who routinely enact actions in accordance with shared understandings of normality and their subjective interpretation of the required forms of appropriate conduct necessary to perform any practice satisfactorily.

On this note, it is instructive to acknowledge that practices are thought to exist both as entities and as performances (Reckwitz, 2002). So first and foremost, the social world is comprised of practices that exist "out there" as recognizable and discernable entities that are configured by a number of different elements. For Reckwitz, these include:

> [f]orms of bodily activities, forms of mental activities, "things" and their use, a background knowledge in the form of understanding, know-how, states of emotion and motivational knowledge (Reckwitz 2002: 249)

There is no universally recognized catalog of the elements that constitute practices as entities but there is tacit and broad agreement that they are composed of objects, materials and technologies; meanings and images; skills and competencies; cultural conventions; social and economic institutions, and spatial and temporal organization (see, for example, Shove and Pantzar 2005; Warde 2005; Shove et al. 2012; Southerton 2013). It is the arrangement and alignment of these "elements" that configure practices as identifiable and intelligible entities. However, it is not enough for practices to simply exist as entities; they need to be performed in order to survive and so the reproduction of practices (as recognizable entities) is reliant on practitioners continuing to enact or perform them in particular ways, and knitting together the various constituent elements in the course of their daily lives. As Elizabeth Shove points out:

> [i]n washing clothes every day, people keep a specific formulation of laundering alive [...] Daily laundering becomes normal, but only so long as sufficient numbers of carriers continue to reproduce it in this fashion. (Shove 2010: 1279)

The distinction between practice as entity and practice as performance is a useful opportunity to consider the place of "the individual" within these theories. In the normal running of things, practitioners (individuals, the carriers of practice) tend to perform existing practices in a habitual fashion and do so consistently and faithfully across space and time such that existing entities are reproduced. However in the course of performing practices, practitioners also tend to "adapt, improvise, and experiment" with ways of doing things and forge new configurations of existing (and incipient) elements. That being so, practices are "dynamic by virtue of their own internal logic" and "contain the seeds of constant change" (Warde 2005: 141). It is through performances—"doings"—that practices as entities are reproduced, modified or otherwise changed by practitioners.

As noted, this line of theorizing has had—following the publication of Alan Warde's landmark article "Consumption and theories of practice"

(2005)—significant implications in terms of how consumption is conceptualized. The consumption of certain things and in certain ways is seen to occur within and for the sake of practices (Warde 2005: 145) meaning that it is a "moment" that arises in the course of doing something else, and that it has less to do with individual attitudes or desires than it does with the shared requirements of accomplishing a satisfactory performance of a particular practice. These insights have particular purchase in policy domains that responsibilize individual consumers. For example in response to the recognition that current patterns of consumption in the global North are environmentally unsustainable, these perspectives suggest that ecologically damaging forms of consumption are not simply a problem of individual consumer behavior. Instead they are understood as being embedded within the prevailing organization of practices which in turn relates to the collective development of what people take to be "normal" ways of life (Shove 2003). Indeed, Elizabeth Shove (2010) notes that a preoccupation with the attitudes, behaviors and choices of individuals has led to the neglect of social science perspectives from outside the "dominant paradigms of economics and psychology" (Shove 2010: 1274). Perspectives that contain a wealth of resources for exploring and better explaining the dynamics of what people do, and then thinking creatively about strategies for affecting change.

It should be apparent by now that public and policy debates about household food waste are not sufficiently attuned to the developments outlined in this section. Hopefully the discussion above provides at least some cause to doubt—or at the very least, not accept at face value—accounts of food waste that are premised on deficiencies in the knowledge and attitudes of individual consumers. This book attempts to account for the ways in which so-called waste behaviors relate to the dynamics of everyday life and so, hopefully, paint a more accurate picture of the reasons why households end up wasting food. Before I get to that, however, I wish to consider perspectives that complement theories of practice but are more ostensibly aligned to material culture scholarship.

BRINGING CONSUMPTION RESEARCH HOME

Within studies of material culture, there is a strong tradition of exploring domestic spaces and processes of home consumption (Cieraad 1999). Much of this work is empirically rich, in-depth and ethnographic, but as Sarah Pink points out: "anthropology *at* home as well as *in the* home challenges traditional ethnographic narratives" (2004: 25) insofar as its subject, method and the researchers' relationship to the field is significantly different to conventional—Malinowskian—approaches. Nevertheless, Daniel Miller has pointed out that anthropology, especially in contemporary industrial societies, needs to go "behind closed doors" (2001a: 1) and engage with the spaces in which "most of what matters in people's lives takes place" (2001a: 3). Allied to this, he has suggested that the home is the primary site (2001a: 239) of consumption, meaning that consumption research—like anthropology—needs to orient itself in this direction and that more generally, a commitment to the ethnographic study of consumption necessitates fieldwork "in the midst of the private domain" (2001a: 239). Researches that have taken up this mantle demonstrate that processes of home consumption are central to the work of personalization and resistance (Miller 1988), social distinction (Southerton 2001), creating the feeling of home (Pink 2012), narrating self-identity, constituting relations of care and devotion and, contemporary forms of mobility (Gregson 2007; Gregson et al. 2007a, 2007b).

More generally, this work provides a welcome rejoinder to some of the more hyperbolic claims that have been made about "consumer culture." It used to be the case that the most influential approaches in consumption scholarship tended to be couched in the rather heady language of aesthetics, identity-formation, desire, hedonism, freedom, representation, domination, manipulation, and ideology. However several decades of social scientific research have now demonstrated that a lot of consumption is rather more mundane and ordinary (see for example Gronow and Warde, 2001).[6] In bringing consumption research home, detailed ethnographic attention has been paid to the process and content of consumption as well as the persons who had hitherto been subsumed under the loaded rubric of "consumers." Again, it is Daniel Miller who has most powerfully illustrated how ethnographic encounters paint a picture in which consumers are neither shameless hedonists nor passive dupes. In a series of reflections on some of the more moralistic theories of consumer culture, he argues that much of what passes for consumption is in fact central to the constitution and expression of meaningful relationships between persons, as exemplified by notions of thrift and sacrifice. To draw on a quote that proves very popular with my students:

> When a mother shops for her child she may feel that there are a hundred garments in that shop that would be fine for all her friends' children but she loves her own child enough that the exact balance between what his or her school friends will consider "cool" and what her family will consider respectable matters hugely to her, enough for her to reject the lot and keep on searching until she finds the one article that satisfies this subtle and exacting need. A woman who feels her boyfriend has paid sufficient attention that he can successfully buy

her a pair of suitable shoes while unaccompanied feels she has a boyfriend to treasure. (Miller 2001b: 230–1)

In short, Miller suggests (2001b) that studies of consumption and our own consumer culture should extend the same patience, empathy, and respect which anthropologists and ethnographers are trained to apply when studying "the other." In doing so, the role of material culture in contemporary societies appears a far cry from the fetishized commodities that lie at the heart of theoretical critiques of materialism and consumerism.

This "grounded form of consumption scholarship" (Gregson et al. 2007b: 188) has made significant progress towards debunking the "myths of consumerism" (Miller, 1995). However as Nicky Gregson points out (2007), once you shift the locus of consumption into the home it becomes clear that consumption is not just about acts of acquisition, appropriation, and appreciation. It is also about "sorting, holding and keeping, and ridding as well" (Gregson 2007: 19) and, as I have elsewhere argued (Evans 2012b), devaluation, divestment and disposal. The bias towards the "front end" (Hetherington, 2004) of consumption, argues Gregson and her colleagues, has led to the retelling of certain myths of consumerism, specifically surrounding "the nexus of consumption, waste and disposal" (Gregson et al. 2007b: 188). One such myth that gets circulated in relation to waste is the idea that contemporary consumer cultures are "throwaway societies." The thrust of these claims is that contemporary cultures are excessive, anomalously profligate, and characterized by a wanton disregard for the material world (see Bauman 2002; Cooper 2005). Against this, Gregson and her colleagues extend the apposite developments in consumption research to questions of divestment and disposal by carrying out in-depth ethnographic research into how households get rid of ordinary consumer objects. They suggest that claims about the throwaway society do not stand up to empirical scrutiny (see also O'Brien 2007; Evans 2012a) by demonstrating that ridding is an "anxiety laden process" (2007a: 684) and that only 29 percent of the discards that they encountered were disposed of through the waste stream. The remainder were handed down, handed around or otherwise saved from wastage (2007a). Gregson et al. deliberately excluded "the leftovers and detritus of food consumption" (2007a: 682) from their study and so the analysis that follows is drawn from a study that was initiated to try and make sense of the undeniable volumes of food that are wasted by households (indeed, this 29 percent is less astonishing once you realize that it does not include food waste) without recourse to the explanations that have gained currency in the realms of formal and cultural politics.

BEHIND CLOSED DOORS

As noted, there is a gulf between social scientific approaches to home consumption and everyday life on the one hand, and the tenor of public and policy debates about food waste on the other. The situation could be characterized as one in which (admittedly alarming) levels of food waste generation are observed and then used as the basis for drawing unsubstantiated inferences and assumptions about why this is happening. As far as I can tell, the Institution of Mechanical Engineers' (IMechE) and the FAO's accounts of why households waste food are not grounded in empirical social scientific research, and so it is hard to view their explanations as anything other than common sense or conjecture. As such, any recommendations for change that flow from these accounts are likely to lead to blind alleys, wrong turnings and dead ends. As Bulkeley and Gregson (2009) point out, there is a need for waste policy and research to engage more thoroughly with "the household, the primary unit of consumption" (2009: 930) and this necessitates a turn to the sorts of ideas presented in this chapter. The book will end with a number of suggestions for thinking differently about strategies for waste reduction and crucially, these will be informed by an altogether different account of, and approach to, understanding household food waste. Rather than observing current volumes of waste generation and reading back to make inferences and assumptions about why it is happening, I take the opposite approach. My research suspends the category of waste (and the judgment that goes with it) and crosses the threshold (Bulkeley and Gregson 2009) to explore household dynamics, processes of home consumption, and the practices of everyday life with a view to understanding the ways in which these result in waste.

In setting out to do the research, it became immediately apparent that ethnography was the most appropriate way to capture what I was interested in. For example, had I tried to administer a survey it would have been very hard not to reproduce the assumptions that underpin existing explanations, or otherwise the assumptions that might underpin an alternative set of hypotheses. Similarly, qualitative techniques such as one-off static interviews would not have been sufficient insofar as respondents are very likely to give socially desirable answers ("no, I don't really waste food") or draw on existing cultural repertoires to explain the food that they waste ("Its BOGOF's[7] isn't it?") More generally, a theoretical orientation towards practice necessitates a focus on "doings" as well as "sayings" (Schatzki 1996) and this commands a methodological approach that locates talk within situated action over an extended period of time. Finally, given the normative connotations of waste, a blunt and one-off encounter with respondents would risk foregrounding certain identities and relations that are not necessarily easy to talk about or comfortable to confront (Hawkins 2006). Aside from concerns about research ethics, my suspicion was that this would make it difficult to recruit and retain respondents and so in order to have on-going access to participants, I needed an approach that looked at waste alongside other—much more benign—household processes.[8] However, as has already been discussed, research that goes behind closed doors challenges traditional conceptions of what ethnographic work entails. Indeed, the difficulties of carrying out research that intrudes into private lives and intimate spaces, and in which ethnographers are more likely to visit their respondents than they are to live with them are well documented (Miller 2001a; Gregson 2007), so too are some possible resolutions of these difficulties (Pink 2004; Pink 2012). It is not my intention to write a detailed methodology section here, but I am frequently asked about the approach that I took to the fieldwork[9] and so it would be something of an omission to not discuss my own strategies for carrying out ethnographic research "behind closed doors" (Miller 2001a).

As a study of material culture, the logic of my fieldwork was to explore how stuff that is understood as "food" ends up as stuff that is "waste" (see also Watson and Meah 2013) and so trace the cultural biography (Appadurai 1986; Kopytoff 1986; Lasch and Lury 1996) of foodstuffs. This involved an approach of "following the thing" (Marcus 1995) and so I focussed on the ways in which households plan and shop for food; how they prepare, consume and eat it; the ways in which they store it, and ultimately, how they get rid of what they do not use. It involved a focus on the very literal movements of food—following it from the supermarket, to the home, to the saucepan, back to the fridge and eventually, the bin. It also involved a focus on the ways in which food moves between categories and evaluations—from raw ingredients, to a cooked meal, to leftovers, to "past its best" and eventually, waste. In order to get at the household dynamics and processes that accompany these movements, I adopted a range of qualitative techniques and the precise mix varied according to what the participating households were willing and able to be involved in. I conducted repeat in-depth interviews with respondents in their homes where we discussed the various ways in which they plan, shop for, prepare, eat, store and get rid of food. Similarly, I retained elements of the classical ethnographic toolkit insofar as I spent a lot of time "hanging out" in respondents' homes, their streets and the neighborhoods in which the study took place. Additionally, I adopted an approach of "going-along" (Kusenbach, 2003) with my respondents in which I participated and observed the things that they would be doing regardless of my presence, and interviewed them *in situ*. Initially, this involved accompanying participants to the supermarket as they gathered their shopping, putting it away with them, cooking with them and on occasion, eating with them. As the study progressed, several respondents invited me to accompany and observe them as they "sorted out" their cupboards, fridges, and freezers. Finally, I made extensive use of cupboard inventories and fridge/freezer rummages as a means of eliciting talk. So for example, in getting respondents to talk about items in their fridge and tracking these over time (e.g. one week's red peppers can become next week's spaghetti Bolognese leftovers), a picture of the social life—and death—of food began to emerge.

Finally, a note on the practical execution of the ethnography, and the people whose lives fill the remainder of these pages. The fieldwork involved sustained an intimate contact (over an eight-month period: November 2009–July 2010) with the residents of two "ordinary" streets in and around South Manchester.[10] In using the term "ordinary," I am signalling that this approach follows Daniel Miller's strategy (1998 on shopping in North London; 2008 on home possessions in South London) of focussing on a particular street and using it as a geographical base from which to conduct ethnographic research in homes and then "spiral out" (Gregson 2007).[11] The two streets that I chose—Rosewall Crescent and Leopold Lane[12]—were selected precisely because I had no particular reason to choose them other than a desire to encounter everyday lives as they are found without recourse to the conventional categories of sociological analysis (Miller 2008). My only criterion was that the streets should be located in areas that—based on my local and residential knowledge—exhibit a degree of heterogeneity, and that the streets themselves should be big enough to reflect that. Both Rosewall Crescent and Leopold Lane are located in areas that I knew to be "mixed" in the sense that they are not affluent suburbs or gentrified areas, nor are they "inner city" estates or districts with high levels of deprivation; rather they sit—sociologically and spatially—between these two poles.

In total, nineteen households participated in the study (eleven from Rosewall Crescent; eight from Leopold Lane) and remained involved for the duration.[13] This sample is by no means representative and I make no claims to generalizability, however the selection of the streets guaranteed at least some variation in terms of income band, age, housing structure, housing tenure, and household composition. I should make clear that this book is not intended to say anything about food waste in different types of household, nor does it seek to theorize or offer explanations along the lines of class, ethnicity, life course, geographical location or any other category of stratification. This is a situation with which I am comfortable (and will return to in Chapter 8) because the purpose of this book is to explore the processes and practices through which "food" becomes "waste," and so offer a rejoinder to the assumptions and inferences that characterize much of the popular and political debate about food waste. Before getting to the substantive chapters and beginning the work of developing this account, a brief note on how these processes and practices will be presented is required.

REPRESENTING THE PASSAGE OF "FOOD" INTO "WASTE"

In presenting their analysis of how households get rid of discarded consumer objects, Nicky Gregson (2007) and her colleagues (2007b) deploy a representational tactic that departs from "an increasingly normative reliance on the use of direct quotation in reporting qualitative research matters in human geography research" (2007b: 199). This same reliance is characteristic of my own discipline (sociology) and in the analysis that follows, I line up with Gregson et al. in starting to move away from this. My approach is to contextualize each empirical example and then switch to a present tense narrative in an effort to evoke a sense of quotidian activities in which persons and things are intertwined. The exception to this strategy is that I remain in the past tense when reporting information that the respondents have narrated retrospectively. The data that informs these descriptions takes the form of conventional field notes, diary records and interview transcripts (see Evans, 2012a for examples of each) but in bringing them together in a common narrative form, I can better convey how the patterning of daily life and the on-going performance of practices works to configure food as waste. The stories that I use by way of illustration are chosen because they exemplify some of the key themes that emerged from my analysis of these data (across all of the households encountered). The chapters that follow unfold in linear succession and so they start with "food" and follow it through sequentially to explain how it becomes "waste." It should be noted, however, that food does not necessarily follow a clear linear passage through the home to end up as waste, and that the analysis will make this clear at various junctures. Nevertheless, this linear narrative is the most appropriate and convenient way of representing the passage of food into waste, especially given the medium chosen to do so (a book). Moreover, the majority of foodstuffs encountered did indeed follow a more or less linear journey and so it is not entirely disingenuous to let my arguments unfold along these lines.

−3−

Contextualizing Household Food Consumption

The participants in this study routinely purchase more food than they are able to find a use for. This is not surprising, however the simplicity of this observation belies its importance in terms of theorizing household food waste. In order to understand how food becomes waste, it is important to first appreciate why households consistently acquire it in quantities that exceed their perceived and immediate requirements for consumption. I am inclined to frame this as a matter of exploring the processes through which food becomes *surplus*, and this chapter begins the work (Chapter 4 completes the picture) of doing so.

My starting point is that notions of "food choice" do not adequately explain why households consistently find themselves in a situation where they have surplus food to deal with. It makes little sense to think that people make deliberate and "irresponsible" choices to purchase too much food when they know that they may end up wasting it. Models of individual consumer choice have long been criticized within social science approaches to food and by way of summary, Shelley Koch (2012) points out that the activity of grocery shopping can be located at "the intersection of individual choice, cultural reproduction, and the larger political economy" (2012: 12). Indeed, it is well established that patterns of food purchasing are an extension of household dynamics and family relations (DeVault 1991) just as observed "food choices" should not be separated from "social influences" (Murcott 1995) such as income, ethnicity and education. More generally, differential and stratified tastes can be identified across different groups of people (Warde 1997). Similarly, the socio-economic patterning of food purchases indicates that there are differences (along the lines of class, ethnicity and geographical location) in access to foodstuffs and by extension people's ability to make "the right" and "responsible" choices (Murcott 2002). Beyond these social and cultural factors, attention has also been drawn to the vertical patterning of food consumption (Fine 1995) and the integration of food production and consumption into broader systems of provision (Spaargaren et al. 2012). This chapter, then, takes a cue from these perspectives on the social, cultural, economic and political contexts of grocery shopping to consider some of the reasons why households end up purchasing too much food.

EATING PROPERLY

In the current cultural landscape, there exists an imperative to cook and eat "properly." It is beyond the scope of this book to discuss where this imperative comes from but "food experts" ranging from policy makers, home economists, and dieticians, through celebrity chefs and advocates, to activists and industry representatives all appear to be playing a role in circulating ideas, definitions and representations of what "proper food" means and entails. For the households encountered on Rosewall Crescent and Leopold Lane, there is a broad consensus around understandings of "proper food" and these are more or less consistent with those identified in the extant literature (see for example Douglas 1972; Murcott 1983; Charles and Kerr 1988; Mitchell 1999; Bugge and Almas 2006; Short 2006; Halkier 2009). These can be summarized as follows: (1) that meals are "proper food" whereas "snacks" are not, but for meals to be understood as such they need to have been prepared—preferably cooked—at home;[1] (2) that meals should be prepared using healthy ingredients as opposed to unhealthy "junk foods" and that ideally, these ingredients should be fresh. In the case of foodstuffs that are positioned as "healthy" (such as fruit and vegetables) but made available in tinned or frozen forms; "fresh" alternatives are understood as better (see also Freidberg 2009) and more in keeping with notions of eating properly; (3) that meals should be prepared from scratch and the logic here is that it is not okay to "cheat" in the kitchen by, for example, using a ready-made stir-in sauce from a jar; and (4) eating properly involves variety within meals (e.g. any given meal should contain several flavors, textures and colors) and across meals (i.e. different things should be eaten throughout the day and meals should be varied from day to day). Allied to this, variety should be experienced by "experimenting" with new foods and a variety of different ethnic cuisines. These understandings of proper food are of course idealized expectations that do not reflect how the vast majority of people go about cooking and eating in their everyday lives. They are nevertheless persistent and carry certain expectations that can be viewed, empirically, as shaping the ways in which people go about doing their grocery shopping.

For example, cooking and eating properly matters profoundly to Sarah—who lives on Rosewall Crescent, is in her early thirties, and is married with two children. Several months in to the study, I was in Sarah's home and having helped wash up after an evening meal, we are sitting and talking with a cup of tea in her living room. The television show "Come Dine with Me"[2] is on in the background and one of the contestants is being criticized by another for using ready-made custard in their pudding (dessert) instead of preparing it from scratch. Sarah's view is that the contestant should lose points for this because they have "clearly cheated." I put it to her that I would not know where to begin making custard if I was not allowed to use custard powder. She responds by suggesting that she tries not to eat or feed her family "sweets" and so has no real need to serve custard, but if she were to do so, she would make the effort to "do it properly." She acknowledges that most people probably do use custard powder most of the time, but also suggests that if you are doing something for a dinner party, then there is no excuse for not at least trying to do things correctly.

Sarah's concern with eating properly is not restricted to special occasions such as dinner parties. It is an imperative that pervades her day-to-day work of household food provisioning. At the time of the study, Sarah had recently returned to work as a result of her youngest child starting school and it is against this backdrop of not spending as much time at home as she used to that she tells me how she is finding it harder to ensure that she and her family eat properly. To this end, she has developed a strategy of using her Sundays to batch-cook several meals for the week ahead. I once spent a whole Sunday with her when she was doing so and throughout the course of the day, it becomes apparent that she is committed to provisioning food in accordance with the understandings and definitions outlined above. At one point early on in the day, she tells me how good it looks to have fresh and healthy ingredients (peppers, lean steak mince, tomatoes on the vine and a bulb of organic garlic) in her refrigerator. These ingredients are later used to prepare a lasagne that takes her several hours to prepare, but which she tells me is worth it because it is easy to re-heat and serve with some fresh salad leaves from the fridge in order to create a "proper meal" that can be prepared with minimal time, effort, and fuss on a weekday evening. With the lasagne underway, Sarah proceeds to make a Moroccan-style chicken casserole (using peppers and garlic already chopped from when she was preparing the lasagne, as well as adding lemon, olives, saffron and other spices). In doing so, she explains to me that it is important to have a variety of different dishes throughout the week and that it is important to have something healthier and lighter than the lasagne. She also suggests that it is good for her children to be exposed to different flavors and cultures from a young age. By the time Sarah finishes preparing these meals and cleaning up after herself, she has committed a large chunk of her day to this activity and is understandably very tired. The fact that she does this almost every Sunday serves to reveal just how important it is to her that she and her family eat properly.

It is instructive to note that the meals Sarah prepares rarely manage to keep everybody in her household fed through to the following Sunday. This is a source of anxiety for Sarah and one of her solutions is to have some "quick fixes" to hand in which she can mix "proper ingredients" together with some "handy cheats" (see also Short 2006)—for example by using fresh vegetables in conjunction with a jar of sauce for a stir-fry. However even allowing for this, her household typically ends up eating what she refers to as "crap food" (for example frozen chicken in breadcrumbs, frozen potatoes, and frozen peas) about once every week. Sarah reasons that if her proper meals and quick fixes can stretch for six days then "one night of junk isn't *that* bad." This hints at a degree of "disconnect" between the ideal of eating properly and the actualities of food provisioning, even for Sarah who undertakes significant measures to the contrary. Unsurprisingly, then, the study brought me into contact with households whose patterns of food consumption exhibit little resemblance to the prevailing understanding of eating properly but even here, the persistence of these expectations is discernable.

For example, Ceri is a single mother of three in her early twenties who lives in a housing trust home on Rosewall Crescent. On one occasion, I was accompanying her as she did her grocery shopping in the supermarket where we spend a lot more time in the frozen food aisles than is the case, for example, when I go shopping with Sarah. Ceri picks up frozen pizzas, meat in breadcrumbs, frozen chips, fish fingers and peas. She tells me that whenever she goes shopping, this is the spot where she fills her trolley up and makes a joke about how little time she spends in the fruit and vegetable aisles. She also confesses that she feels like a "first rate failure" on the grounds that she is "doing it all wrong" and "not living up" to the expectations and instructions she has seen on food-related television programmes.[3] She goes on to explain—both here and during the time that I consequently spend with her—that her life simply does not match this ideal by virtue of a number of factors ranging from her economic circumstances, through her sense that people "like her" are not "into all that" (being a "foodie"), to her children having no interest in eating anything that isn't "pie, chips or pizza." Even though Ceri does not provision food in line with dominant understandings of what it means to cook and eat properly, the fact that she defines herself in relation to—and is troubled by not "living up" to—them attests to their prevalence.

One of the clearest illustrations of how this imperative to cook and eat properly gives rise to surplus food can be drawn from the experiences of Phil and Heather, a married couple in their late thirties who live on Leopold Lane with their two young children. Heather is responsible for the majority of grocery shopping for the household and during one of the occasions on which I accompanied her, some of the tensions she experiences in doing so are revealed. As we walk around the supermarket, Heather reflects on the items that she is putting in her trolley and it becomes immediately apparent that she is concerned with making sure that Phil and her children eat properly. For Heather, this is predominantly a matter of eating fresh and healthy food, and experimenting with a variety of different ingredients and cuisines. However her family are not always receptive to these efforts because her children are "quite fussy" eaters and Phil is quite explicit in his preferences for more traditional foodstuffs ("meat and two veg"). Further, her children will quite happily skip a meal if the alternative is to eat something that they do not want just as Phil will regularly eat out if he decides that he does not want to eat what Heather has prepared. Despite all of this, Heather considers it important for them to eat together "as a family" (Murcott 1997) and so her solution is to continue purchasing the food that she wants her family to eat, but then to purchase additional "fail safe" produce that can be fashioned into "back up" meals if and when Phil or their children refuse the meals that she prepares. Throughout the study, this gives rise to surplus foodstuffs in the form of food that has been prepared but not eaten, and in the form of ingredients that Phil vetoes before they even reach the chopping board. Much of this surplus food is eventually wasted but this outcome cannot be taken as evidence of Heather and Phil not caring. Not only are they both deeply troubled by the food that they waste, but this waste can be viewed as the "fallout" of the other persons (her family) and issues (eating properly, eating together) that Heather cares about, and the ways in which she negotiates these conflicting concerns. At this juncture, it is worth reiterating that the activity of household food provisioning is well understood as a mechanism through which those with responsibilities for grocery shopping (typically mothers) attend to the creation and maintenance of family relationships (DeVault 1991; Burridge and Barker 2009). In particular, the provision of "proper food" allows for the constitution and expression of care and devotion towards significant others (Murcott 1983; Charles and Kerr 1988; Jackson 2009). Additionally, even for those not living as part of a family (however defined), the imperative to eat "properly" connects to broader concerns about healthy living (Peterson et al. 2010) and practising an ethic of caring for the self (Evans 2011a).

ROUTINES

To see how the relationship between understandings of "proper" food and surplus are manifest more generally, it is important to consider the routinized nature of household food provisioning. Marjorie DeVault's influential *Feeding the Family* (1991) locates the work of grocery shopping at the intersection of the household and the market economy, and illustrates how routines develop that extend relations of family and domestic life into commercial spaces such as supermarkets. In the majority of households encountered, the work of grocery shopping is heavily routinized insofar as it tends to take place at relatively fixed intervals (it varies across households but it is commonly every seven to ten days) in the form of a "big shop" at a large out-of-town super-market.[4] I was able to accompany several respondents doing their grocery shopping on more than one occasion, and so observe that they each tend to follow a fixed route through the supermarket and purchase roughly the same things each time that they go. The routinized nature of grocery shopping, however, is not always a good fit for the rather more fluid ways in which lives are lived and this mismatch can result in food—especially "healthy" items—creeping into the category of surplus.

This can be illustrated through reference to the workings of Kirsty and Tony's household. Kirsty and Tony are a married couple in their mid thirties with two children who have been living on Rosewall Crescent for around five years and proudly identify themselves as lifelong residents of Manchester. Both Kirsty and Tony think it is important to eat healthily and to this end, they deliberately purchase "healthy stuff" when they go to the supermarket. However in common with many households, they often end up not eating these healthy items—especially fruits. At one level, this can be viewed quite simply as the gap between "good intentions" and real life. Certainly they report specific instances of *not* eating apples, peaches, grapes, bananas and clementines that they had in the house because they fancied a chocolate bar or bit of cake instead as a snack or their "something sweet."[5] In Kirsty's own terms, they have "healthy weeks" where they eat all of the fruit that they purchase, but they also have "bad weeks" where they do not. Either way, they always purchase the healthy items because more often than not they will eat them, and they do not know "in advance" if they are going to have a "bad week." Further, Kirsty suggests that it is important to keep fruit in the house on the grounds that they would never eat it if she didn't[6] and that the guilt she experiences when she throws it out makes her try harder for the whole family to eat healthily the following week. Although the routine acquisition of fruit intermittently leads to instances in which it becomes surplus, these occurrences are not easy to anticipate, nor is the routine easily modified in response to the imperatives of waste reduction.

A more general point can be made here. The prologue to this book discussed how broccoli comes to be wasted in Sadie's home and part of the story was that the leftover half got displaced when a newer, fresher, whole broccoli was acquired. The purchase of foodstuffs that go on to replace and displace items already in the home (and already running the risk of not being eaten) is common to every household that I encountered, and the routinized nature of grocery shopping goes a long way to explaining why this happens. Staying with Tony and Kirsty, an example can be drawn from an occasion on which I went grocery shopping with Kirsty. Kirsty is doing a "big shop" because it has been "about a week" since she last did one and they are running low on supplies that need to be replenished in order to feed the household over the following seven to ten days. However, they have not run out of everything that they will need and as it happens, they still have a number of items in the fridge—including half a bag of satsumas and a whole, unopened, packet of green beans—that could still be used. Under normal circumstances, these items would have already been eaten in between shopping trips, but over the last week something has happened to prevent them from doing so. Kirsty speculates that this might have been a parents' evening (parent-teacher interview) but she cannot say for certain. Anyway, we do not realize that these items are still in the fridge until we return from doing the grocery shopping and so in the supermarket, Kirsty purchases a new bag of satsumas and a new packet of green beans. Her reason for doing so is that, quite simply, she tends to purchase the same things each time that she goes shopping. As she puts these items into the fridge, their older counterparts go into the bin because, as is the case with Sadie's broccoli, Kirsty knows that there is no way that she will be able to find a use for the "old" satsumas or green beans, nor is she willing to jeopardize the new foodstuffs in order to salvage the old ones.

My argument here is that things become surplus in ways that are more closely connected to the routinized nature of food provisioning than to the conscious evaluation of individual foodstuffs.[7] Campaigning efforts to reduce food waste attempt to intervene in these processes of routine over provisioning by advising households to check what is already in their kitchen before doing their shopping or better still, to move away from doing "big shops" at the supermarket in favor of buying what is needed, when it is needed, from local food retailers. This is certainly good advice and the participants in this study are certainly aware that "it would be sensible" to put it into practice. However not everybody has equal access to these local shops and in actuality, people tend not to shop in this way especially when they are having to juggle multiple demands (for example work, parents' evenings or socializing). Further, there is no denying that the emergence of large out-of-town supermarkets has engendered a degree of convenience in helping to organize and enact the flow of daily life. I highlight this in order to emphasize that the ubiquity of the supermarket has less to do with the preferences of individual consumers than it does with the ways in which modern modes of living have collectively been developed. For example it connects to patterns of housing, planning and development; labor market trends and societal divisions of labor (including domestic divisions of labor); technological and infrastructural innovations and, the temporal pulse of contemporary societies. I am certainly not attempting to suggest that supermarkets should be absolved of responsibilities for tackling food waste at the level of the household; rather I am trying to suggest that some of these other issues should not be overlooked. That said, I turn now to one of the ways in which they are directly implicated in shaping the conditions that lead to households routinely acquiring surplus food.

INFASTRUCTURES OF PROVISION

As noted, the vast majority of participants do the majority of their grocery shopping in the supermarket, and the most significant contribution that this makes to the acquisition of surplus foodstuffs relates to the ways in which retail practices shape patterns of home consumption.[8] Overwhelmingly, the households encountered experience relatively little control over the quantities in which they purchase food. Throughout the study, wasted food was articulated in terms of having no choice but to purchase —for example—a packet of three mixed peppers when one would have sufficed, having to purchase a 300 gram tub of hummus when only a few dips were required, or only having the option to buy a large bag of bean sprouts when the recipe only called for a handful. Several respondents despair at the perversity of only being able to buy foods in excessive quantities and so frequently wonder out loud as to "who on earth?" would ever need or be able to use up all of the food acquired in the portions that supermarkets make it available. However, beyond simply drawing on these repertoires of justification in order to make excuses when confronted with the food that they are throwing out, these concerns are manifest (and empirically observable) in all of the ways that they provision food (shopping, preparation, eating, storage and so on). For the purposes of this section, however, it is instructive to consider them specifically in relation to the activity of grocery shopping.

For example, Julia is a married woman in her early thirties who lives with her husband and two young children on Rosewall Crescent. In one of my first meetings with Julia she was very enthusiastic about inviting me to talk through the items in her fridge. Almost immediately, we come to half of a cauliflower head that was left over from making a cauliflower cheese the previous week, and she readily admits to not knowing what to do with it. It isn't that she is short of ideas for what she *could* do with it or that she is lacking in culinary skills; it is just that she and her family only like cauliflower when it is "smothered" in cheese and as such, she is mindful that they don't eat too much of it. According to Julia, "although it [cheese] is delicious" it is also "really fatty" and she wants to make sure that her family "stay healthy." She also discusses her worries about the food that she purchases but does not find a use for and to that effect, she actively tries to purchase food in quantities that are a better fit for her patterns of use. I witness this when I accompany her as she does her grocery shopping in the supermarket. She picks up a whole cauliflower head and alludes to our earlier encounter, stating that it would be much better if she had the option to buy half the amount. She concedes that this probably wouldn't make much sense because this is the quantity in which "nature makes them." Moving on, she goes in search of carrots. She picks up a large bag of carrots and comments that she knows that she will not use them all up before they start to go off and resolves to find the "loose" items so she can purchase the three or four that she realistically anticipates a use for. We circle the fruit and vegetable aisles several times searching for the loose carrots but in the end, Julia asks a member of staff where to find them and we are informed that the only option is to purchase the whole bag of carrots. More generally, several respondents actively seek to purchase food in more appropriate quantities, for example: single lemons instead of a bag with six in, a smaller bag of salad leaves, or a pack with two bagels in rather than five. However, more often than not, these efforts are unsuccessful, leaving people no choice but to purchase too much of an item or else not purchase it at all.

It should be noted that these frustrations apply to most categories of food and drink including dairy, dried goods, tinned foods, stir in sauces, bakery produce and to a lesser extent, meat. However they are most clearly pronounced in relation to fresh fruit and vegetables and here, the connections between food surplus and food waste are most keenly felt. Certainly the respondents report a good deal of anxiety about "keeping on top of it all"—finding a use for foodstuffs that are surplus to requirements and demanding to be eaten within a particular time-frame by virtue of their perishability. This anxiety is brought about at the intersection of the quantities in which supermarkets make food available (infrastructures of provision) and prevailing notions of what it means to cook and eat "properly." Further, it is these same understandings and definitions of "proper food" that prevent households from reducing the amount that they waste by adapting their practices to better fit with the quantities in which food is made available to them. For example Sarah suggests that she would waste less food if she were the kind of mother that "goes to Iceland"[9]—by which she means using a lot of frozen food (pizzas, burgers, fish fingers and so on) to feed her family. However she also suggests that she just could not do this insofar as it would be tantamount to not eating properly. On the topic of using frozen vegetables (which in theory could circumvent some of the difficulties that arise when attempting to find a use for their more perishable counterparts), she suggests that they are "okay" but that there is no substitute for using *fresh* vegetables, and that she would rather not compromise.

Returning to Julia's efforts to purchase smaller quantities of carrots, she briefly entertains the possibility of purchasing a mixed bag of pre-prepared (but fresh) vegetables (carrots, cauliflower, broccoli and peas) but dismisses this option. Julia's objection has nothing to do with the relative cost of these bags (which she suggests will entail paying more for less), rather she views their use as tantamount to "cheating"—the antinomy of cooking properly and so an unsuitable vehicle for constituting familial relations of care and devotion. Finally, this concern with eating properly and its role in the acquisition of surplus food is not unique to persons with responsibilities for feeding the family.

For example, Tamsin is in her mid twenties, describes herself as "terribly middle class" and lives alone in a one-bedroom apartment on Leopold Lane. Her employment requires her to travel away from Manchester frequently meaning that she "does not know where she is going to be from one moment to the next." When I first meet Tamsin she explains that she tries to cook and eat properly when she has the chance, but the problem is that recipes often call for "five different ingredients" that she can only purchase in quantities that exceed her requirements. This means that she is often left with "five lots of stuff left over" that she is liable not to eat by virtue of her erratic schedule. In a later interview she tells me that her solution is to batch cook meals, put them in the fridge and heat them up when required, enabling her to treat "proper food" as convenience food, and so overcome some of her difficulties in scheduling everyday life (Warde 1999; Southerton 2003). However she also confesses that this does not work because she does not like eating the same meal several nights in a row. As is the case with Sarah's rejection of frozen food and Julia's refusal to use pre-prepared vegetables, this is not an individual disposition; it is one that chimes with shared conventions and in this case, it is a matter of associating variety with good taste.

In sum, this chapter has demonstrated that there is no single factor that explains why households shop for groceries in such a way that a certain amount will inevitably slip into the category of "surplus." I have suggested that grocery shopping needs to be understood in relation to household routines, shared understandings and definitions of proper food, and the ways in which supermarkets make food available. Further, I have argued that it is the intersection of these factors that begins to explain how and why households purchase more food than is required for their immediate requirements of consumption. In order to develop my account of how food becomes "surplus," the following chapter explores how the routine over provisioning of food connects to the ways in which households negotiate the complex and contradictory demands of everyday life.

–4–

Anxiety, Routine and Over-provisioning

In discussing how food becomes surplus, the previous chapter necessarily glossed over some of the things that households could be doing in order to slow or prevent these movements. It would be entirely reasonable for you to be thinking that it shouldn't be that difficult to find a use for half a cauliflower head, or that it wouldn't take much effort to do a bit of planning and so cut down on the acquisition of surplus foodstuffs. In this chapter, I suggest that things are rarely this straightforward and demonstrate some of the reasons why the passage of food into the category of surplus might be impervious to campaigning efforts that seek to modify household and consumer behavior. More generally, I discuss (following Meah and Watson 2011; Watson and Meah 2013) the ways in which conflicting social anxieties are negotiated into practices of domestic provisioning and the routine enactment of daily life. With this in place I summarize the ideas presented in Chapters 3 and 4 to develop a position on how food becomes surplus, and so lay the ground for Chapters 5, 6 and 7 to explore how "surplus" becomes "waste."

FAMILY AND KIN RELATIONSHIPS

It is important to recognize that observable household behaviors such as the act of wasting food are not reducible to the actions of individual consumers. The previous chapter highlighted the role of cultural conventions (eating properly) and commercial infrastructures (the quantities in which super-markets make food available) in structuring household processes of surplus acquisition. However the household itself is not a unified and singular actor in the food system, and it is well understood as a site through which family and kinship relations are performed and negotiated. For example, it is well established that those who assume responsibility for feeding the family tend to subsume their own tastes and preferences to those of others in their household. Traditionally, this has been theorized in relation to women taking their husband's desires into account (Murcott 1983; Charles and Kerr 1988) but more recently, attention has been drawn to the whims and wishes of children (Burridge and Barker 2009; Koch 2012). These dynamics have powerful impacts when it comes to thinking about food and surplus. For a start, there is the common sense (which is not to say inaccurate) observation that people over provision because they would rather make too much food available for others to eat than for there to be too little. This ethic of generosity is an appropriate mode of expressing care towards significant others and by contrast, it would appear stingy to not make sufficient food available. Similarly, I have already given the example of Heather whose enduring commitment to commensality and ensuring that her family eat properly underpins the provisioning of "back up" meals to make sure that her family have enough to eat. By definition, this involves the acquisition of surplus foodstuffs (see Evans 2012a).

It is useful to consider the ways in which these family dynamics intervene to prevent people from finding a use for surplus food. It is often assumed (see Chapters 1 and 2) that the problem is one of domestic deskilling and a more charitable variation on this theme can be found in WRAP's *lovefood-hatewaste* campaign. The campaign website allows households to specify the food that they have left over (e.g. prawns, cherries, leeks) and then search for appropriate "recipes" and suggestions on how to find a use for the item selected.[1] I do not dispute that this is a useful resource (not least because I often make use of it myself), but initiatives such as this perhaps overlook the extent to which a lot of people often have very clear ideas about how they could fashion meals out of the ingredients that need using up. This is certainly the case for many of the respondents encountered and here, the burden of surplus does not often stem from a lack of culinary skills or knowledge; rather it relates to the domestic context in which food is provisioned.

For example, Suzanne is a single mother in her thirties who lives on Rosewall Crescent with her two children. She is highly skilled in the kitchen, understands a lot about food and is more than capable of improvising to create meals out of whatever is in the fridge. However on one occasion about half way through my fieldwork, we are rummaging through her fridge and we get to a bag of spinach that has about a quarter of the contents remaining. This leads to a discussion in which Suzanne explains to me that if she lived on her own, she would be willing and able to cook something quick and easy—perhaps an omelette—that would use it up. However she goes on to explain that she does not live alone and that her children are "fussy buggers" who would not be particularly impressed were she to give them a spinach omelette for their evening meal.

As she laughs about this, she clarifies that they are not *that* fussy insofar as they will try new things (and over the course of the study, I witness Suzanne successfully introduce new dishes to the suite of meals that they will accept), but that they have a clear preference for "tried and tested recipes"—things they have eaten before and enjoyed. In the end, she does not prepare a spinach omelette nor does she use the spinach in preparing the evening meal. She instead prepares penne pasta (she would prefer to use spaghetti but her children are not yet able to eat it without making a mess) with a Puttanesca sauce[2] (in which she uses less chillies than she would like because her children have "not yet developed a taste for hot stuff"). Suzanne's food provisioning activities are located—in common with many respondents—within a context where there is a relatively fixed culinary repertoire and other members of the households will only eat certain things. Given that Suzanne's children are not overly receptive to new concoctions, especially "improvised" meals, it is perhaps not surprising that she goes for a "tried and tested recipe" instead of attempting to cook something that would use the spinach up. However as a consequence, the spinach remains surplus to requirements meaning that it is at risk of becoming waste.

PLANNING

It is often suggested that if households were to plan their grocery shopping and consequent patterns of food consumption more meticulously, then they would reduce the amount of food that they waste. At first glance this appears to make perfect sense, however I am inclined to suggest that households already do a good deal of planning, and that it would actually be quite hard to plan for the contingencies that render a certain amount of food as surplus to requirements. The respondents encountered—especially those living as a family—can be viewed as approaching the task of household food provisioning with a high degree of organization and planning.[3] Admittedly, very few could be said to plan what will be eaten meal-by-meal, day-by-day or to reflect this by putting detailed information on kitchen notice boards and refrigerators. However this does not mean that they are not planning, and a real advantage of the ethnographic method is that it reveals the more subtle and taken-for-granted approach that many households have to planning and food provisioning.

For a start, I have already mentioned that households tend to do their grocery shopping at relatively fixed intervals (typically every seven to ten days) and that they tend to purchase the same, or at least similar, set of items each time that they do so. On the other side of this equation there is a tacit expectation—recalling the aforementioned preference for tried and tested recipes (see also DeVault 1991)—that certain things will be eaten at some point, if not a fixed point, in the intervening periods between shopping trips. To the extent that the content of meals varies, it is understood that certain ingredients can be turned to multiple purposes. For example, minced beef can function as the basis for a chilli-con-carne one week, and then the basis for a cottage pie the next. All other things being equal, this equation should balance out into a "functional equilibrium" (Jackson et al. 2013) such that households do their grocery shopping when they have used up the food acquired during the previous trip, and that all of the items purchased for use within a given time period will be eaten before going shopping again. However all other things are not equal and these plans—which in theory have the potential match acquisition to use—are thrown out of balance by the rather more fluid nature of the ways in which lives are lived.

In the previous chapter, I hinted that it is this intermittent and erratic "mismatch" between acquisition and use that reconfigures food that would normally be eaten, as food for which there is no immediate use. In terms of how this relates to surplus, the disruptions to the normal running of things are likely to entail the acquisition of additional foodstuffs—typically outside of the home—that will be eaten in the place of food already purchased. So, for example Sadie—whose broccoli opened this book—is extremely diligent in her planning of meals and organizing the schedules of the various members of her household, however disruptions to the ordinary running of things can move food seamlessly into the category of surplus. Rummaging through her fridge on a Monday afternoon, we discuss an unopened packet of four pork chops that would normally have been eaten the previous Wednesday or Thursday. However her son had been taking part in a martial arts competition the previous Thursday and the whole family had watched him compete before going to Pizza Hut to celebrate his success. This is not something that happens every week and Sadie points out that even though she knew that this was going to happen, it is not the kind of thing that she carries "at the front of her mind" when she does the grocery shopping, meaning that she did not adjust her purchasing accordingly. If disruptions to the routine enactment of daily life can lead to the acquisition of surplus food in a very organized household such as Sadie's, then it is perhaps not surprising that it happens when things come up more generally—having to work late, getting stuck in traffic, having an unexpected visit from an old friend or a family member—in other households.

Indeed, these processes are particularly apparent in households that are inherently more chaotic than Sadie's. It will be recalled that Tamsin's experiences of household food provisioning are characterized by a sense of "not knowing where she will be from one week to the next." It is this sense of dislocation that underpins her routine acquisition of surplus food. When Tamsin has been working away from Manchester, she tends to forget what—if any—food she has in her fridge and cupboards. She explains to me that when her train pulls into the station, she is tired, hungry and "in desperate need of food," and so she ends up either purchasing something "quick and easy" from the supermarket (a ready meal or a bag of salad), getting a takeaway or arranging to go out for dinner with a friend. As the previous chapter demonstrated, Tamsin very often has "five sets of leftover ingredients" lying around from her efforts to cook properly when she is at home, and so all of these options involve purchasing additional items when it is likely that she already has food that could be eaten. However this is perhaps less a matter of Tamsin being careless and choosing not to find a use for the items that she has already purchased than it is a consequence of the temporal pulse of modern life intersecting with the aforementioned demands of cooking and eating "properly." Aside from people not necessarily having the time to cook "proper" meals from scratch; a lot of so-called "proper" food imposes its own demands in terms of the time frame within which it must be eaten. Specifically, fresh food is very often unforgiving insofar as the temporalities of its decay render it unable to accommodate erratic work schedules such as Tamsin's. For reasons of being tired and hungry, or not being able to remember what is in her kitchen—all of which are perfectly understandable—food that has already been purchased gets displaced and moves into the category of surplus.

In a slight variation on a theme, the ordinary running of things is something that households might actively and intentionally disrupt—precisely because they are so mundane. Further, they might do so in ways that involve the consumption of additional foodstuffs that in turn displace items that they had already acquired and planned to eat. For example, I encounter several instances in which Kirsty takes the opportunity to eat outside of the home and so "skip" meals or snacks that could have been fashioned out of the items already in her kitchen. The first time that I accompany her to the supermarket, we are loading bags of groceries into the trunk of her car but before driving back to her house, she rummages through the bags looking for a multi-pack of crisps (potato chips). Upon finding one, she seeks out her favorite flavor (salt and vinegar), asks if I want to choose a pack for myself and then locks the car. As we sit enjoying our crisps, she tells me that this is a treat that she allows herself when doing the grocery shopping. She also points out that she would get hungry if she did not do this and that this packet of crisps will "see her through to the evening," meaning that she will now not eat anything else for lunch today. To see how this connects to surplus, it is instructive to recall that Kirsty is a housewife who spends a lot of time at home, and whose lunch is usually fashioned from the leftovers of the previous evening's main meal. In eating the crisps and skipping lunch, the leftovers that would normally constitute her lunch slip into the category of "surplus."

On another occasion, having carried out an interview with Sadie, I go to a "greasy spoon"[4] that is a short walk away from Rosewall Crescent in order to get something to eat, write up some field notes and pass the time before returning to carry out another interview. Sitting at my table, I see Kirsty walk into the takeaway section of the café and I smile at her by way of saying hello. She throws her arms up, starts laughing and announces "you got me" before explaining that she often comes in here on the days that she has no other reason to leave the house. Again, she talks about this in terms of treating herself but also in terms of "getting out of the house" and needing to "feel part of the world." In a later interview, she refers to this encounter quite explicitly in the context of a discussion about how she occasionally breaks her routine of eating leftovers for lunch (Evans 2012a). One might wish to argue that Kirsty *could* stay at home, eat the leftovers and so prevent them from becoming surplus to requirements. However arguments such as these—quite aside from lacking humanity and empathy—miss the point that as a "housewife," Kirsty is structurally at risk of boredom and isolation (Oakley 1974; Pink 2004). Her desire to take respite from the home and the work of household management is perfectly understandable and although food becomes surplus (and at risk of becoming waste) as a result of this; I struggle to accept any interpretation that rests at attributing blame to Kirsty.

In all of these examples my argument is that in the ordinary running of things, there is a "match" between patterns of grocery shopping and patterns of food consumption, and that this can be understood as a routine that evolves so that households can manage the competing pressures on the organization of daily life (Jackson et al. 2013). For many sociologists, it is almost axiomatic to view such routines as a form of "practical consciousness" (Giddens 1984), and my suggestion here is that it is not easy to adapt these deeply entrenched patterns of grocery shopping in response to sporadic disruptions whether they are anticipated, unexpected or even deliberately pursued. Additionally, observable patterns of food consumption can be viewed as the outcome of the various demands that are placed on the practice of domestic food provisioning including the differing tastes of family members, household budgets, calorific intake and the imperative to eat properly. Here, it is important to emphasize that concerns about wasting food (and money) are common to virtually all of the households encountered and that the evolution of routines that seek to match patterns of grocery shopping to patterns of food consumption can be interpreted as a reflection of this (Evans 2011a, 2012a). It is only when things go out of balance—which of course they do very frequently, albeit in varied and unpredictable ways—that food becomes surplus and so edges closer to becoming waste.[5] However, it is also important to recognize that concerns about food waste intersect and come into conflict with other concerns around feeding the family and managing the household. It is to these issues that I now turn.

ANXIETY, THRIFT AND HYGIENE

Throughout the study, a good deal of anxiety was reported and observed around the act of wasting food. During interviews, fridge rummages, shopping trips, and the preparation of meals, respondents frequently tell me that it is "wrong" to waste food and that they feel "guilty" or "terrible" when they end up doing so. Beyond simply telling me how bad they feel about wasting food, these concerns are very clearly manifest in the ways that they go about attempting to prevent waste, recover surplus food, and extend the process of ridding. Chapters 5, 6 and 7 will explore these processes in more detail but for now, two things in particular are of note: (1) that despite these anxieties; all of the households encountered continue to waste food in quantities that appear to resonate with the national estimates offered by WRAP (2011); and (2) that in articulating these anxieties, only one of the households encountered does so through reference to the environmental impacts associated with wasting food (see Chapter 1). Accounts that invoke the perversity of throwing food away whilst distant others are starving, or wasting food that something might have died for (in the case of animal produce) are slightly more common. However, overwhelmingly (see also Watson and Meah 2013) there is a sense in which respondents understand food waste as a failure in household management (see Evans 2012b) that connects to concerns about wasting time and wasting money, as well as a more abstract and general conviction that food is something that should not be wasted (Evans et al. 2013a).

In their analysis of household food provisioning, Matt Watson and Angela Meah (2013—see also Meah and Watson 2011) suggest, "a host of potential social anxieties can be part of what gets cooked up in the domestic kitchen" (2013: 98). Focussing specifically on food safety and food waste, they illustrate the ways in which these concerns are manifest in public and policy discourses before suggesting that they pull the activity of domestic food provisioning in conflicting directions. Through empirical engagement with household performances of food consumption (with a particular focus on use-by date labelling) they demonstrate that their respondents exhibit standards of food safety that fall short of those inscribed in policy recommendations. More importantly, they argue that as households negotiate these conflicting concerns into practice, they open up moments in which stuff that is food "crosses the line" to become stuff that is waste. With this, they argue that food becomes waste through everyday practices, "the convergence of diverse relationships" (2013: 112) and the displacement of concerns about food waste by other—perfectly legitimate—concerns about food safety. My own fieldwork and analysis leads to similar conclusions, however I am inclined to suggest that food rarely crosses the line to directly become waste, and that it must first move into the category of surplus. This subtle distinction intimates a slightly different account of how social anxieties underpin the generation of food waste. Before getting to that, it is worth reflecting further on how anxieties about food safety help food in crossing the line to become surplus.

For a start, I have given examples of how the activity of grocery shopping involves the acquisition of new foodstuffs that displace their older counterparts by facilitating the *acknowledgment* that they are surplus to requirements. Even though the older items might immediately get placed in the kitchen bin and so apparently cross the line to become waste, it is likely that the aforementioned disconnect between patterns of grocery shopping and the flow of everyday life had rendered them as surplus before they were recognized as such. It is not difficult to see that public discourses about food safety help to facilitate and legitimate the acknowledgment of certain items as surplus, and so send them in the direction of the waste stream.

For example Faye and Chris are a couple in their late twenties who rent a one-bed apartment in a converted block on Leopold Lane. On one occasion, having been grocery shopping with them, they are sorting out their fridge and making room for their newly acquired foodstuffs.[6] For Faye and Chris (in common with some of the households already discussed), this involves getting rid of certain items when there is a newer counterpart ready to hand with which to replace them. On this occasion, they throw out a lone green pepper, half a tub of stir-in carbonara sauce and what remains from a block of cheddar cheese. They both appear troubled by this but Chris draws attention to the "state" of the items that he is pulling out of the fridge, compares them to their newer counterparts and suggests that it is better that the former are thrown away now than to risk wasting the latter at some point in the future.

At this point, Faye interjects to point out that this is particularly true given the increased potential for the older items—which have been "kicking around a while," are "a bit skanky," and "past their best"—to make them ill.

More generally, the households encountered here were found to be negotiating similar concerns about food safety and storage into their practices of domestic food provisioning (Watson and Meah 2013). Every respondent stressed that when food starts going bad or begins to go "past its best," it is likely to be less safe and so less fit for human consumption than it previously was. Further, they were particularly keen to emphasize this point when they had a newer and safer alternative with which to replace it. The application of this logic works to categorize—or at least acknowledge—certain foods as being surplus. Of course, the ways in which respondents evaluate food as "past its best" varies across households and according to foodstuff. For example some households rely on use-by dates and labels whilst other prefer to "trust their nose." Some evaluate food according to its aesthetic qualities (discoloration, "drying out") whilst others consider how long it has been sitting unused in their fridge, freezer or cupboard. Some foodstuffs are understood as highly risky (meat, poultry, fish, and dairy) whilst others are understood as more "forgiving" (onions, herbs, and spices). Despite these variations, the unifying feature across households and in respect of all foodstuffs is the idea that food's potential to make people ill accelerates—and legitimizes—evaluations of food as surplus to requirements. Similarly, concerns about food safety tend to override those about food waste such that public discourses of health promotion (in this case, ensuring that unsafe food is not eaten) are being negotiated into practices of domestic provisioning in ways that enable "food" to cross the line to become "surplus." Please note that I am not critiquing discourses of food safety and storage, I am simply illustrating how they help to create the conditions through which food becomes surplus.

At this juncture, it is worth exploring the ways in which households delineate the categories of "new" and "old" food. Overwhelmingly, newly acquired groceries appear to belong to a category that is distinct from existing foodstuffs already in the kitchen and destined to become surplus. Further, there is a sense in which items from these discrete categories should not be mixed together because of the potential that exists for the older foodstuffs to pollute or contaminate the newer produce.

Returning to Chris and Faye and continuing the encounter discussed above, they explain to me that they very often face a situation in which they acquire a new tub of carbonara sauce when they still have a half-eaten one left over from a previous shopping trip. The reason for this is that a whole tub contains the right amount of sauce for both of them but if one of them isn't eating at home, the other will still make penne carbonara, but only use half of the tub. Chris tells me that if they are both eating penne carbonara, he would never entertain the prospect of mixing the leftover sauce with half of the new tub; he would simply use the whole (unopened) tub of the new sauce meaning, of course, that the old one is acknowledged as being surplus to requirements. Faye elaborates on this by suggesting that if they were to mix half of the new tub together with the remainder of the old one, there would be a risk of rendering the "whole lot" unfit for consumption. Her reasoning here is that "you have to be careful with cream and milk" and if the old sauce is "on the turn," then combining the two might lead to them having to throw away "the perfectly good [new] stuff" as well. Here Chris muses that they probably feel the same about the "wrinkly" green pepper that he doesn't think would pose any risk if it were to be chopped up and mixed with one of the new peppers. Faye confirms that they have never, and probably never would, mix these items together at which point, Chris concludes—and Faye agrees—that there is something "not quite right" about mixing old and new items, and that it is "one of those things" that they "just don't really do." The polluting effects of the surplus, then, appear to extend beyond the potential—whether real or imagined—for food that is going bad to make people ill and into the symbolic realms of the domestic cosmology.

To unpack this further, it is useful to give some more detailed consideration to the ways in which anxieties about food waste are articulated and experienced in practices of domestic food provisioning. Returning now to Watson and Meah's analysis, they suggest that anxieties about wasting food do not readily connect the global social and environmental consequences, and that "[m]ost concerns seem closer to home. Rather than an expression of global citizenship, resistance to wasting food is primarily rooted in *thrift*" (2013: 109 emphasis in original). Following Miller (1998, 2001b), they conceptualize thrift as the simultaneous expenditure and conservation of finite resources—typically money—in ways that allow for responsible management of the household and the expression of care and devotion towards significant others within the home.[7] I certainly agree with their assertion that anxieties about wasting food are rooted in thrift and that in turn, these connect to concerns about good kitchen management and responsibilities to the household. However returning to my aforementioned departure from their analysis, I am minded to suggest that these anxieties are more closely aligned to the routine acquisition of surplus and that—somewhat counterintuitively—these anxieties about surplus can play out in ways that lead to the wastage of food. So as already mentioned, the households encountered are clearly troubled by the act of wasting food, however many of the examples above signal that also—and perhaps ahead of this—there are moments in which they become troubled by the presence of surplus food. Indeed, surplus food is a material reminder that something has gone wrong (or at least not according to plan) vis-à-vis the efficient management of household resources, and confronting its presence brings about this acknowledgment and recognition.

On this note, it is instructive to consider the broader historical processes that underpin prevailing notions of good household management. Gavin Lucas (2002) argues that modern domestic economies are characterized and caught between the twin moral systems of thrift and hygiene. Moreover he suggests that issues of waste and disposal can be analyzed in relation to these systems and the ways in which the tensions between them play out in the material culture of the home. The analysis above certainly supports this conjecture insofar as surplus food can clearly be understood as unhygienic by virtue of its potential to render other food inedible or to make people ill. However it suggests that surplus food can also be viewed as dirty in the more symbolic sense famously identified by Mary Douglas (1966) insofar as it represents a disruptive presence within the home when judged against the imperative to manage the household in line with the principles of thrift, economy and efficiency. The removal of this material, then, can be viewed as an attempt to restore order to the household economy whilst offering up the potential for a fresh start—to try again—with the new intake of groceries. Viewed as such, it becomes apparent that in addition to preventing food from "crossing the line" to become waste (Watson and Meah 2013); anxieties about food waste and their articulation in relation to thrift can play an active role in directing food towards the waste stream.

SUMMARY

Before exploring the management of surplus in more detail, it is worth pausing to summarize the arguments that I have made over the course of the previous two chapters regarding the ways in which "food" becomes "surplus." I have argued that the routine acquisition of surplus food cannot be reduced to a matter of "food choice" or irresponsibility on the part of individual consumers, and that it arises at the intersection of a number of determining factors. Attention has been drawn to cultural conventions, the historical evolution of how people shop and manage their homes, commercial infrastructures of provision, household dynamics and the material qualities of food itself. Further, I have suggested that the competing pressures on household schedules and the work of domestic food provisioning means that routines of food consumption are not readily amenable to the rational and deliberate models of intervention that policy makers and campaigners are currently deploying in order to reduce household food waste. Taken together, my position is that "food" becomes "surplus" as a result of processes that have little to do with "waste" or consumers actively seeking to over-provision on the grounds that they do not really care. Rather, surplus is presented as normative and as something that occurs in the course of households doing other things. Although surplus food is far from benign in its consequences, it is rather more mundane in its origins—it is the fallout of everyday life—and it is important to take stock of this before moving on to see how it may or may not go on to become "waste."

–5–

The Gap in Disposal: From Surplus to Excess?

Understanding how "food" becomes "surplus" is only half of the story. It is an important first step in tracking the passage of "food" into "waste," but it is not a foregone conclusion that surplus food will go on to become food waste. However, as will be seen, the households encountered overwhelmingly manage the disposal of surplus food in ways that lead to its wastage. Despite this unfortunate conjunction of disposal and waste, there is, at a theoretical level, no automatic equivalence between surplus things, their disposal, and the creation of waste matter. This chapter follows surplus food into a "gap," and introduces some of the conceptual and empirical resources required to start making sense of the processes through which surplus food crosses the line to become waste. In doing so, I theorize the process of ridding in more detail, explore the possibility of recovering food from the category of surplus and address the uncertainties surrounding the onward trajectory of things that have fallen into the gap in disposal. With this in place, the stage is set for Chapters 6 and 7 to explore the ways in which the ridding of surplus and excess foodstuffs is enacted once they have passed through this gap.

THE PROCESS OF RIDDING

In its broadest sense, the term disposal invites a focus on the ridding of surplus things, however it tends to automatically conjure up images and associations—usually negative (see Chapter 1)—of "waste." Reaching beyond this common sense and narrow interpretation, there is an important distinction to be drawn between the act of wasting and the *process* of ridding (Gregson et al. 2007a). Clarifying these concepts yields two very important insights. Firstly, that the disposal of surplus things does not necessarily involve or lead to their wastage. Work by Rolland Munro (1995) and Kevin Hetherington (2004) makes a theoretical plea—recalling canonical anthropological writings (for example Malinowski 1922; Mauss 1954—for recognition of the multiple conduits that societies develop to enable the re-circulation or disposal of surplus things. It will be recalled, also, that Gregson et al.'s (2007a 2007b) empirically grounded analysis of discarded consumer objects suggests that they are very often disposed of through conduits that save them from wastage (for example donations to charity shops or "handing down" to friends, neighbors and relatives), with only 29 percent disposed of in ways that route them in the direction of the waste stream. Secondly, that whichever way households ultimately end up disposing of discarded materials; the process of ridding is enacted gradually (Lucas 2002) insofar as surplus things are not immediately placed in conduits that lead directly to their disposal. Viewed as such, observable acts of wasting—such as those that underpin current volumes of household food waste—need to be understood in the context of broader and more complex processes. Chapters 6 and 7 deal with the workings of the multiple trajectories through which discarded food might potentially be disposed of, but this chapter focusses on what happens in between food becoming surplus and its eventual placing in one of these conduits of disposal.

Surplus things are inherently ambiguous. On the one hand, they are not immediately useful and have not yet realized the value that was anticipated at the point of acquisition. On the other hand, however, they are not useless nor are they devoid of the potential to be re-valued given a different set of circumstances. So whilst they are surplus to the perceived and immediate requirements of household consumption, their residual sources of use and value have not yet been exhausted and so it would be inappropriate to categorize them as "waste." This is perhaps not surprising insofar as the classic essays on the social life (Appadurai 1986) and cultural biography (Kopytoff 1986) of things have long recognized that any given object will be assigned different values and uses as it moves in and out of its different phases, and is exchanged between different users. It follows, then, that it would make little sense to think of commodities (including food) going simply from being usable to non-usable—or from valuable to waste—without hesitation or complication. In practice, things are rarely disposed of at the point at which they are acknowledged as surplus; rather they are put somewhere else such as in the attic, the shed or the garage, or perhaps in a box under the bed or at the back of the wardrobe. These interim placings work to suspend surplus things between presence and absence in the home and punctuate the work of disposal such that it is enacted via a two-stage holding process (Lucas 2002). Kevin Hetherington (2004) suggests that this creates a "gap" in disposal through which households deny the wastage of things whilst they attempt to obtain settlement with the value that remains.

The trajectories of foodstuffs encountered in this study can be said to involve passage into the gap in disposal, and this assertion rings true across the spectrum of categories that constitute surplus food. For a start, it applies to food that has not been cooked, opened or otherwise prepared, and is surplus by virtue of being unused "ingredients." For example, in conversation with Julia she explains to me that she feels stressed out when she has food in the kitchen that she cannot find a use for. She confides that she has developed a strategy in which she "forgets" that these surplus ingredients are there (she makes the inverted comma gesture with her hands to signal that she is actively rather than passively forgetting) until they reach a point at which they have passed their best, and she can throw them away "with an easier conscience." However she rarely manages to *actually* forget about these surplus items. Indeed she will tell herself—and throughout the study, tells me—that she will find a use for these items later in the week such as "a stew or something." Despite these intentions, she often ends up not doing anything with these ingredients and so feels "bad," "sick," and "angry" with herself for letting them go to waste, indicating that her strategy is not as effective in easing her conscience as she might like it to be.

The leftovers of foodstuffs that has been cooked—or at least eaten—in the home tends to undergo a similar process, except here the interim placing that marks the gap in disposal is easier to discern. Rather than simply remaining in the fridge or the cupboard, these surplus foodstuffs are physically placed there and are very often covered (with tin foil, cellophane wrap or an upturned plate) or otherwise contained (for example, by emptying them into a Tupperware box). For example, Tom is in his mid twenties and lives alone in a converted flat on Leopold Lane. He works long hours in IT and so tends not to cook or prepare food at home. Instead he eats out, eats at work or in the event that he is eating at home, gets a takeaway. Whilst talking through the items in his fridge, he spots a plastic tub that is roughly two thirds full of rice and draws my attention to it by exclaiming that it is "pretty rank." Discussing it in more detail, it turns out that these are the leftovers of a Chinese takeaway that he had acquired about a week ago. He had purchased a portion of rice to accompany a pork and black bean dish and although he ate all of the pork in one sitting, he needed only a small amount of rice to go with it. Consequently, he waited for the remaining rice to cool down, put the lid back on the tub and placed it in the fridge in order to keep open the option that he could return to the takeaway at a later date, buy a main dish and use the leftover rice as an accompaniment. However, in the course of our discussion he tells me that he has probably never eaten rice out of the fridge and begins to think out loud that "you are not meant to heat rice up" before placing it in the bin. In both of these examples, the gap can be viewed as something that extends the process of ridding, both spatially (in these cases to incorporate the fridge as well as the bin) and temporally (in the sense that there is a period of time in between the point at which things become surplus and the point at which they are ejected from the home).

Tom's example relates specifically to surplus takeaway food, however the process can readily be applied to the leftovers of meals that have been prepared in the home. There is an important distinction to be drawn between leftover food that has been prepared but not served (such as the remains of a casserole or an oven-baked lasagne) and that which is left over after people have eaten (such as food left on a plate or milk left at the bottom of a cereal bowl). Where surplus foods that have not been served can unproblematically enter the gap in disposal in much the same way as Chris's rice; food that has touched a plate or been part of somebody's meal is much more likely to bypass this process and end up directly in the bin. At this juncture it is instructive to acknowledge the trajectories of things that do not follow the route of becoming "surplus" and entering the gap in disposal. In the course of the study, I encounter numerous instances in which potentially edible matter is immediately discarded and placed directly in the bin. In addition to the broccoli stalks mentioned in the prologue, these include: the crusts from loaves of bread, fruit and vegetable peelings, chicken carcasses[1] and the fat from cuts of meat such as pork chops[2]. These direct connections between edible matter and the bin are most apparent during my observations of food preparation. This is perhaps not surprising insofar as food preparation can usefully be viewed as an activity that involves the separation of "food" from "non-food," and it follows that stuff that does not enter the category of food is not then going to follow the same trajectory as stuff that does. Indeed, stuff that is "non-food" does not go on to register as "food waste" from the perspective of the households encountered, even though these cultural demarcations are unlikely to reflect what actually counts as food in a medical sense (Murcott 1993) or indeed, what counts as wasted food from a material flows perspective. My intention in noting this is not to proclaim ignorance or profligacy on the part of the household; I am simply signalling that the line between food and non-food (e.g. that British people tend not to eat broccoli stalks) is very much a matter of cultural convention.

I will reflect further on the categorization of "food" and "non-food" in my discussion of how things exit the gap in disposal to enter conduits that may or may not lead to their wastage. However before getting to this, there is a need to return to empirical examples and consider what happens once this gap in disposal has been opened up, and to then consider how things might be recovered from the category of surplus to unambiguously become "food" again.

RE-ORDERING

As noted, the gap in disposal extends the process of ridding—both spatially and temporally. Thinking back to Chapter 4, this extension can usefully be interpreted as unveiling household anxieties around having to get rid of surplus food. The fact that households do not immediately get rid of surplus food suggests that they are following particular procedures in order to manage its disposal effectively and appropriately. Indeed, the presence of this gap in disposal suggests that reported household anxieties about wasting food are more than empty words insofar as they are manifest (and empirically observable) in domestic practices. It is important to recognize, however, that the gap is not simply the spatial and temporal extension of the kitchen bin (and the attendant acts of wasting), rather it is a complex terrain in which households attempt to obtain settlement with the residual value of surplus food whilst hoping to resolve ambiguities and questions about the extension or termination of its social life. Accordingly, it is useful to consider what goes on in domestic kitchens once this gap in disposal has been opened up. The best way of doing this is to follow surplus food into the gap and present empirical material that illustrates the household processes that accompany the time that it spends there.

For example Natalie is a divorcee in her mid forties who owns her own hair salon and lives in a semi-detached house on Rosewall Crescent with her two teenage sons. One Thursday, I accompany and observe Natalie as she prepares a chicken, chorizo, and chickpea casserole that she describes as "easy enough to prepare," "something that everybody enjoys," and a "good solid meal." The surplus that is left over as a result of cooking and eating this meal includes roughly one third of the casserole that was not served up,[3] a yellow pepper (she used the red and green peppers from a mixed packet of three), half a small tub of cream (the recipe doesn't call for it but she likes to add a little) and a small amount of fresh parsley. This surplus does not include the non-food that she immediately discards during food preparation (for example the stems, seeds and white membranes found on the interior of peppers) nor does it include the ingredients (such as the one and a half red onions left in the pack of three that she purchased) that she can readily find—and has already planned—a use for ("they'll be used for a lasagne on Monday, I always make a lasagne on Monday"). The ingredients listed above are "surplus" because as they were purchased specifically to make this casserole, but recalling the arguments put forward in Chapter 3, Natalie could only purchase them in quantities that exceed the quantities in which she requires them. Anyway the pepper, the cream, and the parsley are placed immediately in the fridge (in the vegetable tray, the milk shelf and on top of the eggs respectively) during the preparation of the meal. The casserole is left in the pan to cool on the stove or in case anybody wants second helpings during the meal. After the meal, Natalie places the lid on top of the pan and we do the washing up together. She tells me that she isn't going to put the pan in the fridge because it is far too big and she anticipates that one of her sons will eat it when they get back from college the following afternoon, and that it will be safe to leave it at room temperature for a short period of time. By the time I leave Natalie's home, the surplus of this meal has entered the gap in disposal.

I return to Natalie's home the following Monday because this is her day off[4] and she has agreed to let me accompany her as she does the grocery shopping. Looking through her fridge, I notice several things: (1) that the cream is no longer there; (2) that the leftover casserole has been transferred into Tupperware containers and placed on the bottom shelf; (3) that the parsley has been transferred to a re-sealable airtight bag; and (4) that the yellow pepper has been moved up to the middle shelf. Taking each of these items in turn, Natalie begins by telling me that she threw the cream away after a couple of days. She had tried to think of what to do with it, including having it in her coffee or getting a pudding (such as a lemon tart) in especially to eat with it. She had even tried giving some to her cat "as a treat" but as it turned out, he wasn't that interested. In the end, she decided that she would rather not eat unhealthily or purchase additional food that she doesn't really want just to find a use for this cream, and that the cream was probably past its best having been open for a while. As for the casserole, her sons did not eat any of it on the Friday (as she expected they would) and she explains that this meant that it needed to be moved into the fridge so that it can be "kept good" for longer. She also tells me that nobody has eaten any of it since it went in the fridge and speculates that this is because she doesn't always remember what's in there and her sons are unlikely to look "any further than the ends of their nose." Moving on to the parsley, Natalie informs me that this has been placed in an airtight container because it was starting to look "a bit wrong" from not being properly covered up (initially it was left in the original packet that had been torn open) and that she wants to preserve it because she is planning to give it to one of her customers who is coming in the following day, and who has previously expressed an interest in trying out Natalie's casserole recipe. She also confides, however, that she is worried that it might be "a bit odd" or even awkward to give "some dying parsley" to somebody that she doesn't know very well. Finally, the pepper has been moved out of the fruit and vegetable tray at the bottom of the fridge and onto the middle shelf because it is much more visible there. Here, Natalie returns to the point that she often forgets what is in the fridge and suggests that by moving it out when she remembers (she moved it on Saturday), she will remind herself to try and do something with it.[5] Her plan on this occasion is to stir it into the ragu sauce that will provide the basis for the lasagne that she will make later on. Natalie suggests that ideally, she wouldn't use peppers in this sauce but reasons that it will be hard to notice them and it will make sure that they get used up.

Thinking now about the eventual fate of these items, the cream—as noted—was already placed in the bin but interestingly, most of the other surplus foodstuffs ended up there too. Some of the casserole was eaten but the remainder—in keeping with the logic of prolonging its life through preservation by domestic technologies—was moved into the freezer where it remained uneaten at the time of the study finishing.[6] In the end, Natalie decided against giving the parsley to her customer and so having held onto it for another "week or so," she felt that it was best to "let it go." Finally, as she chopped the pepper to put in the lasagne, she decided that it had gone "too slimy" and so scraped it off her wooden board and into the bin. Although the vast majority of this surplus food actually went in the bin, this simple observation obscures the extent to which food is moved, handled and thought about upon entering the gap. Again, this can usefully be interpreted as a practical manifestation of anxieties about how to manage its disposal. Clearly, then, a lot happens within the gap. Things are physically moved around in order to preserve them, remember that they are there, entertain potential uses and set these ideas in motion. Equally well, these movements can involve things being buried, hidden, and actively forgotten to momentarily deny their wastage whilst simultaneously rejecting the possible futures that have been conjured up. Either way, after a certain period of time, surplus food emerges from the other side of the gap in order to be disposed of in one way or another. However, there also exists the potential for surplus to be retrieved from the gap and to re-enter the category of food that is fit for the perceived and immediate requirements of household consumption.

RETURNING

The gap in disposal is not a black hole. It would be disingenuous to suggest that all surplus food follows an irreversible and linear trajectory in which passage into the gap marks a point of no return. The above example of Natalie's yellow pepper illustrates how surplus food can start to move in the other direction and although in this particular case, it doesn't quite succeed in crossing the line back into the category of "food;" there are several instances in which other items do.

For example Laura is in her late thirties and lives in a large house on Rosewall Crescent with her partner James and their three children. One Wednesday evening, I am in Laura's kitchen as she prepares a chicken curry and upon opening the fridge to get some chilli peppers, she spots an unopened and unused cauliflower head. She tells me that this has been there for well over a week and that James had purchased it intending to do something with it. He had forgotten that he was due to go away for work the previous Thursday and Friday and so was not around to cook the meal that he had planned. Pulling it out of its packaging she squeezes it, smells it, inspects it and concludes that it is "on the turn." She nevertheless places it on the chopping board and cuts the florets off the head (immediately discarding the stem) and starts to tell me that she wouldn't normally put cauliflower in a chicken curry—she would most likely use broccoli or another green vegetable—because it doesn't look quite right, but in the interests of "using it up" she concludes that it will be fine. When it is time to add the cauliflower to the pan, she stirs in roughly one third of what she has cut and the rest goes into the bin. I ask her how much broccoli she would normally put in this dish to which she replies that she would put about the same amount as the quantity of cauliflower that she used, but would only prepare and remove the florets that she intends to use. She explains that because she is going to dispose of the cauliflower that she does not use, she is making the whole thing available so that she has the option of saving more of it from wastage. Two things are of note here: (1) that once again movements, placings and materials (in this case, the chopping board and the knife) are used to extend the gap in disposal in much the same way as was the case with Natalie's pepper; and perhaps more importantly, (2) that at least part of this surplus cauliflower is recovered from the gap in disposal to be used as food.

Another example can be drawn from my encounters with Pete. Pete is in his early twenties and lives with four other people that he describes as "a bunch of randoms" (room mates that he didn't really know until moving in with them) in a shared house on Leopold Lane. His work requires him to be

away from home frequently and like Tamsin, this sense of instability charac-
terizes his accounts of food provisioning. Unlike Tamsin, however, he is in a
position to make use of surplus food as a means of feeding himself. In my
first meeting with Pete, we are standing in his kitchen and he picks an apple
out of the fruit bowl, offers one to me and proceeds to tell me that these are
not "strictly speaking" his to eat or to give. Picking up on my awkwardness
about having already accepted one, he starts laughing and explains that
every week the girls (Kate and Louise) that he lives with[7] purchase "loads
of fruit" but then go on to eat "probably about 30 percent of it." Gesturing
towards the fruit bowl, he tells me that they purchased nine apples five days
ago and that they have only eaten one each since then. He also tells me that
this happens all the time and that about a month ago, he decided to just
start eating their fruit because it saved him from having to buy his own and
that in any case, he was "getting sick of things going to waste." I ask if they
mind him eating their fruit to which he replies that he doubts that they would
even notice and that they haven't mentioned it yet if they have.[8] Effectively,
food that becomes surplus for Kate and Louise is retrieved from the gap that
they have created by Pete.

Pete's recovery of surplus food is not, however, limited to eating things
that other people have purchased. Indeed he jokes that "leftovers" are one
of his favorite meals and gives examples of the "odd mish-mash" of things
that he has eaten on occasions when he returns home from being away and
"cannot be bothered to sort something proper out." For instance he details
how he had recently put together a three-day-old madras (hot curry) sauce
(leftover from a takeaway) with sausages from the supermarket, some bread
that "was looking a bit old" and the "sweaty" remains of a bagged salad. For
Pete, recovering surplus food from the gap in disposal obviates the need for
another meal to be prepared when he has neither the time nor inclination
to do so. He is by no means alone in viewing surplus food as a potential
resource to be mined when the opportunity arises.

For example Caroline is in her early sixties and a long-term resident of
the neighborhood in which Rosewall Crescent in located. She shares her
home with her husband, Daniel, and although her three children are all grown
up; her daughter and one of her sons live very nearby. Caroline's daughter
and daughter-in-law regularly "pop in" at short notice during the day and on
these occasions, she "pulls something out of the freezer"—such as leftover
portions of shepherds pie, moussakas or pasta bake—for them to eat. She
tells me that she views these as a godsend as it means that she only has
to put them in the microwave or the oven to re-heat[9] thus leaving her free to
have "quality time" with her family. She suggests that preparing even simple

meals such as toasted ham and cheese sandwiches would detract from time that she would rather be spending with her loved ones. Caroline is very close to her family meaning that these visits are valuable, however this closeness means that she does not feel embarrassed about not preparing "something special" for them, and that in any case (she is chuckling as she tells me this), they all claim to love her cooking. She also confesses that she would throw these leftover portions out if they were left uneaten in the freezer for more than a couple of months and so she is glad that she has the opportunity to use them up, and for somebody to enjoy them.

Despite these examples of surplus being recovered from the gap in disposal, it should be noted that Pete and Caroline are not typical of the participants in this study. Across the vast majority of households and foodstuffs encountered, the overwhelming tendency is for food that becomes surplus to follow a linear passage through the gap, and to come out the other side to be disposed of through one conduit or another. Chapters 6 and 7 will discuss the workings of these different trajectories but before getting to that, it is important to consider the ways in which different things are routed into these different trajectories.

MOVING THINGS ALONG

The account of disposal that is being developed here is one that conceptualizes it as "not primarily about waste but about *placing*" (Hetherington 2004: 159 emphasis added). It follows that waste is not an innate characteristic of certain things or things in a certain state; rather it is a consequence of how the disposal of surplus things is enacted once they have been released from the gap. For example, disposing of surplus things by gifting them to friends and family will more often than not save them from immediate wastage whereas placing them in a bin or taking them to the tip is likely to connect them directly to the waste stream. Returning now to the work of Nicky Gregson and her colleagues and their assertion that only 29 percent of the consumer discards that they encountered were routed through the waste stream with the remainder being placed in conduits that save from wastage; it is useful to consider how and why different things end up following such different trajectories.

In a debt to Georges Bataille (1985), Gregson et al. (2007a 2007b) draw a useful distinction between surplus and excess. Surplus things are thought to have the potential to be valued elsewhere such that their social lives (Appadurai 1986; Kopytoff 1986) can be extended by moving them along

(Gregson et al. 2007b). The category of excess applies to objects that cannot be imagined in terms of this productive expenditure on the grounds that they are ""disgusting," "worn out," and "shot through" (Gregson et al. 2007b: 198). This distinction implies that surplus things will be placed in conduits that keep them out of the waste stream (charity shops, eBay, friends and relatives) whereas the best or perhaps only option for excess things is for them to be placed in conduits (typically the bin) that will set them directly on course to being placed somewhere (typically landfill) that configures them as waste. Transposing this distinction into my sketch of how "food" becomes "waste," it implies that "surplus" things become "excess" before they become "waste." To formalize: if surplus things become excess then they will be disposed of in ways that constitute them as waste; however if they remain in the category of surplus, they will exit the gap to be disposed of in ways that save them from wastage. As will be seen, surplus food slips rather readily into the category of excess and is therefore routinely placed in conduits that lead to it becoming waste.[10] However, there is nothing inevitable about this and so the following chapters explore these processes in more detail and consider why alternative conduits do not operate consistently or effectively to dispose of food in ways that disrupt its passage into waste.

–6–

Bins and Things

This chapter considers the overwhelming tendency for surplus foodstuffs to be cast as excess and then placed in conduits that send them in the direction of the waste stream. Leaving aside (for now—the following chapter returns to these issues) consideration of why alternative conduits do not operate consistently or effectively to enact the disposal of surplus food in ways that save it from wastage, the analysis here pays attention to the connections between surplus food and food waste. Central to this is a discussion of bins and the role that they play in stabilizing the trajectories that lead to the wastage of surplus food. I suggest that this stability is—at least in part—a consequence of the bin's agency, the unique materiality of food and the ways in which these elements align with the material culture of the home more generally. In developing this argument I attend to two further issues. First, the ways in which the representational effects of surplus and excess things interact with these material processes in order to shape the topographies of disposal. Second, the ways in which this analysis of bins and disposal relate to the possibilities of food recycling schemes.

FROM SURPLUS TO EXCESS

Having argued that "food" becomes "surplus" (Chapters 3 and 4) and then enters the gap in disposal (Chapter 5), it is important to now theorize its exit from the gap and its placing in conduits of disposal. The vast majority of foodstuffs appear to slip from "surplus" to "excess" whilst being held in the gap such that it becomes appropriate to place them in the bin, which in turn routes them through the waste stream. Acknowledging these movements helps to explain—albeit in the abstract sense—the steps that "food" follows *en route* to becoming "waste." At this juncture, it is instructive to consider empirical examples of how "surplus" slips into the category of "excess." The previous chapter detailed Julia's strategy of quietly but actively forgetting surplus food and waiting for it to go "past its best." To explore this process in more detail, consider the following diary entry in which she kept a record of the food that she had thrown out in a given week:

- a small amount of sundried tomato paste
- three bananas
- quarter of an iceberg lettuce
- one beetroot
- half a block of feta cheese
- about one pint of milk

I ask her why she threw each of these items away and she begins by telling me that the tomato puree had been "drying up a bit" and looking "dodgy" for a while, but that she had held onto it in case she had the chance to "throw it in" a pasta sauce to mask the decline in quality. However once it started to visibly go mouldy, she knew that she would not eat it and so threw it in the bin—along with the jar that contained it. I put it to her that she is normally such an avid recycler and she responds by suggesting that the jar was "too dirty" to go in the recycling.[1] Moving on to the bananas she tells me that the first one that she threw away was originally one that she had taken with her to work, only to discover that it had gone "mouldy and brown" in a number of places when she peeled it in preparation for eating. Returning home, she checked the two that remained from a bunch that she had purchased the previous week, decided that they were in a similar state and so put them straight in the kitchen bin. In the case of the lettuce, Julia explains that it was starting to show specks and spots of brown, which for her means that it is "probably off" and that the flavor will certainly be affected to the point that she is no longer willing to eat it.

In her discussion of the beetroot, Julia opens her fridge and pulls out a packet of four cooked beetroots that have been vacuum-sealed and informs me that the item that she threw out was the remaining item in a pack like this. She explains that although she thinks that these are a great product—cheap, nutritious and tasty—she also finds them to be a real problem because if you do not eat all four in one sitting, they are "a bitch to store," not least because the "juices leak everywhere." On the occasion in question, she had drained the "juices" from the packet and put the remaining beetroot in a Tupperware container with the intention of using it for a salad later in the week, however it had "dried out" and "started smelling odd" very quickly. She reasons that they probably need to be stored in the liquid if they are to be preserved and so in the absence of said liquid, she placed the beetroot in the bin. She reports a similar set of problems with the feta cheese.

Julia loves feta cheese but is annoyed that it "leaks all over the place" as soon as the packet is opened. Her solution is to put the packet directly in a Tupperware box and then open it, thus ensuring that the cheese and the liquid are suitably contained. However, despite her best efforts, she finds that it quickly starts to smell and look "really bad" meaning that if she doesn't eat it all within a few days of opening the packet, she will have to throw out what is left. Here—and this applies to her explanation of the milk that she wasted as well—Julia feels that one has be very careful with dairy produce, predominantly by virtue of its potential to make people (her, her family) ill but also in terms of it making her fridge (and by extension, her kitchen and home) smell bad, and in terms of it being "disgusting" when she has to sort it out. For example, she describes being "close to vomiting" when she pours milk that has gone off or the liquid from the feta cheese down the drain, and so she holds her breath and immediately "chases" it with bleach before washing her hands thoroughly.

Julia's stories encapsulate processes that I observed consistently across all of the participating households. To develop this insight in a more theoretical register, the snapshots above can usefully be interpreted as surplus food becoming excess whilst it is held in the gap in disposal. It will be recalled that excess things are understood as "disgusting," "worn out," and "shot through" (Gregson et al. 2007b: 198), and so cannot be imagined as useful or valuable. Indeed, Julia's reaction to the feta cheese and milk is visceral, embodied, and affectual[2] just as the glass jar that held the mouldy tomato puree is contaminated to the point of overriding an otherwise diligent commitment to household recycling—simply by being in contact with excess matter. Effectively, then, the slip from "surplus" to "excess" marks the point at which food is no longer food (by extension, and contrast, this means that surplus food is still food insofar as it can and indeed might be eaten). This is not to dispute that the distinction between "food" and "non-food" is complex and contingent, and dependent on a host of medical and gastronomic factors that vary across time and space (Murcott 1993; see also Coles and Hallet 2013).[3] What is important, however, is that when households categorize something as "non-food"—no matter how subjectively—they demarcate it as "excess" and this is consequential insofar as the item in question is sent in the direction of the waste stream.

Thinking with the theoretical framework developed by Michael Thompson in his book *Rubbish Theory* (1979), food can be viewed—in common with most consumer objects—as a transient thing insofar as its value decreases over the course of its lifespan until it slips into the category of rubbish (zero perceived value). However unlike other objects, the lifespan of food is relatively short and so it reaches the rubbish category relatively quickly and once there, it is unlikely to be rediscovered, or to enter the category of durable (stable or increasing) value. This rapid passage and inability to escape the category of "rubbish" is conceptually analogous to the slip from "surplus" to "excess" and it implies that questions of value can be resolved—at least in part—by not disposing of food at the point at which it becomes socially obsolescent. Holding surplus food in the gap in disposal allows for it to be quietly but actively forgotten in an effort to ameliorate anxieties around overprovisioning[4] and attendant perceptions of poor household management. Keeping it around on the grounds that it might be used in the future not only means that "a respectable interval has passed for any residual value to be passed on" (Hetherington 2004: 170) but also that processes of physical decay work to support those of symbolic devaluation and so facilitate the "slip" of surplus food into the category of "excess," at which point it becomes possible to manage its disposal through the waste stream via the act of placing it in the bin.

It is important to re-iterate that it is by no means a foregone conclusion that *all* surplus food entering the gap in disposal will exit as excess, get placed in the bin and consequently routed through the waste stream. However, again, it is the common trajectory of the foodstuffs encountered here and it is consistent with current estimates of household waste generation in the United Kingdom. At first glance, this suggestion appears to run counter to studies (Gregson et al. 2007a, 2007b) that attest to the effective workings of alternative conduits. By way of reminder: Nicky Gregson and her colleagues estimate that just 29 percent of discarded consumer objects are routed through the waste stream with the remaining 71 percent disposed of through conduits that save them from wastage. However, it will be recalled that they did not include food in their analysis and crucially, that they account for materials routed through the waste stream by drawing the distinction between surplus and excess things. Viewed as such, the findings here are entirely consistent with their analysis insofar as food emerges as a particular genre of material culture that slips rather readily, rapidly and frequently into the category of excess. I turn now to a discussion of what it is about food that makes this so, and the role of material culture in shaping the connections between surplus food and food waste.

MATERIALIZING TRAJECTORIES, STABILIZING CONDUITS

Food—unlike the consumer objects in Gregson et al.'s study (2007a, 2007b)—is particularly susceptible to rapid spoilage and decay, meaning that there are significant risks (whether real or perceived) associated with its consumption. Indeed, every household that I encountered stressed that food that has gone mouldy, gone off or otherwise "gone bad" cannot be eaten and has to be thrown out. As such, foodstuffs are particularly well suited to claims that objects do not have fixed properties or qualities (Ingold 2007), but rather are in constant flux and becoming (Bennett 2007). The generation of food waste cannot be understood solely as a consequence of human activity insofar as all manner of biota and microbes play an active role in facilitating the slip from surplus to excess, from food to non-food. These processes of physical transformation and self-alteration suggest an active vitalism (Bennett 2010) that animates (Bennett 2007; see also Hawkins 2006) food and in doing so, creates certain affordances in practices of disposal (see also Gregson et al. 2010). As has already been noted, the presence of surplus food is a source of anxiety for households by virtue of its representational effects. It can now be argued that the dissipative materiality of food (Bennett 2007) and its physical manifestation as mould, discoloration, changes in texture and so on renders it complicit in calling forth its own ejection from the home. Accepting that this disposal is enacted in ways that connect it to the waste stream, food itself can be viewed as a relevant actant in shaping its own passage to becoming waste.

This line of analysis invites further reflection on why it is that food is consistently disposed of in ways that configure it as waste. Part of the answer will have to wait until Chapter 7, where I discuss the paucity and inefficacy of alternative conduits of disposal, however it can be noted here that bins play a significant role in finalizing the transformation of food into waste. Returning to the idea that surplus and excess foodstuffs are a troublesome presence in the home, bins offer up the possibility of "sealing off" the offending materials. For example during one of my early encounters with Chris and Faye, they inform me that it "bugs" them if there is food in the kitchen that they know is probably not going to get used. During this discussion, Faye walks over to their kitchen bin,[5] lifts the lid up and places it down again. She explains that when something goes in there, it is "basically game over" and "like admitting defeat"—accepting that the food in question will now definitely not be eaten, at least not by them. No matter how much they dislike throwing food away, Faye nevertheless suggests that putting it in the bin means that they no longer have to worry about it, and that they can "move on to worrying about something else." As Nicky Gregson and her colleagues point out, bins operate to "[r]eclaim the self from the polluting effects of the excess" (Gregson et al. 2007b: 196) and as will be seen in the following chapter, placing it in alternative conduits would risk carrying these polluting effects forward.

Allied to this, bins can be viewed as materializing waste relationships at the interface of private households and public systems of waste management systems (Chappells and Shove 1999). Crucially, the kitchen bin connects discarded food with material infrastructures and institutions of collection and disposal in a manner that does not require too much effort on the part of households.[6] Having sealed themselves off from the polluting effects of surplus and excess food; households need only to ensure that their "rubbish" is placed in an appropriate place, and at an appropriate time, for it to be collected and carried away by an external and public agency. Several respondents report that once stuff is "out for collection" it both belongs to, and is a problem for, public systems of waste management. So where Faye suggests that she no longer has to worry about food once she has put it in the bin, the act of doing so makes it something to be dealt with by somebody else, outside of the home. Of course once the "rubbish" is out for collection; it is on a direct route to becoming "waste" because this stream will most likely be headed for landfill or incineration. To borrow an idea (following Hetherington 2004) from Hertz's (1960) analysis of funeral rites, the social death of food can be thought of in terms of being marked by a "first burial" (in the bin) followed by a second or final burial in which it is laid to rest in landfill, its transformation to "waste" complete.

It is important to remember that although the bin operates effectively as a conduit through which to dispose of surplus and excess food, the removal of an object from the home does not necessarily eradicate its semiotic presence, nor does it prevent the material absence from "acting back" in a representational sense (Munro 1995). These "ghosts" of unmanaged disposal (Hetherington 2004: 170) represent unresolved questions of value and so even if households only put surplus food in the bin after its sources of value appear to have passed on, they still report and experience anxieties around its onwards trajectory into the waste stream. For example, I have already detailed how Julia's efforts to "actively" forget food are not particularly effective in easing her conscience. Elsewhere in the study, she articulates that the reason she still feels bad is that she thinks that she "should" or "could" have found a use for the surplus food placed in the gap, or perhaps planned better to prevent its acquisition in the first place. Similarly, despite Faye's initial assertion that placing food in the bin makes it somebody else's problem; she nevertheless expresses concern about what the local authority will then do with it, especially as she suspects that it will go straight to landfill. The effects generated around the semiotic presence of food that has been physically disposed of amount to anxieties around its wastage, and that something might have been done differently at the level of the home or household to avoid this outcome.

Hauntings aside, the point remains that bins and associated waste management systems are very good at getting rid of surplus and excess matter. Current volumes of household food waste can in part be explained by the observation that bins work consistently to effectively enact the disposal of food. The stability of this conduit—in contrast to the ones discussed in the following chapter—derives from the various non-human (biotic and abiotic) actants that hold it together. The analysis above highlights the alignment between food as an unbecoming material, the bin itself, and infrastructures of collection and disposal. Accepting that the act of binning is the outcome of a more complex process of ridding, the role played by a range of other devices comes into focus. Indeed, the gap in disposal is made possible by a range of domestic technologies such as fridges, freezers, and Tupperware containers, as well as less obvious materials such as aluminium foil, chopping boards, and knives. It is well established that domestic technologies play a dynamic role in relation to practices of home consumption (Shove and Southerton 2000; Pink 2004; Watkins 2006; Silva 2010) and here, it can be noted that items designed (or at least marketed) for the preservation of food can, in actuality, operate as coffins of decay that play an active role in carrying discarded food towards the bin. In sum, my argument is that non-human elements help to manage anxieties around the presence of surplus food in the home, allow for the conflation of its representational and material effects, sustain the normativity of binning it, and provide an effective mechanism for carrying it off to its final resting place.

FOOD RECYCLING

In recent years, an increasing number of municipal and local authorities in the U.K. have rolled out infrastructures intent on capturing surplus and excess food, and diverting it from landfill. This change in waste relationships at the interface of private homes and public systems of waste management is manifest in the form of the food recycling bins (or "caddies") issued to households alongside instructions on the arrangements that are in place for the collection of their "food waste." Having argued that the stability of the trajectories connecting surplus food to the waste stream depends largely on the material agency of the bin, it seems logical to take an optimistic view of these initiatives. Indeed they appear consistent with the analysis above and can be interpreted as an attempt to work with the affordances of the bin to materialize a conduit that keeps discarded food out of the waste stream. In theory, this approach allows households to place matter that they have categorized as excess in the bin but then—in keeping with the idea that "waste" is a matter of placing and not a fixed characteristic of certain things—diverting it once it is in the hands of waste management systems. I will be addressing policies and initiatives for waste reduction in the concluding chapter but for now, the centrality of bins to the argument at hand necessitates a parallel discussion of food caddies. I should note that my research was unable to pay sufficient attention to these devices because at the time of the study they were only available to the residents of Leopold Lane, and were only introduced towards the end of my time in the field. Nevertheless it is striking to note the myriad ways in which households are responding to them and that in particular, many seem to be resisting and refusing them.

Firstly, however, it is important to recognize that several households actually welcomed these caddies as a useful intervention in their food waste practices. For example, on one occasion I was in Faye and Chris's apartment having been grocery shopping with Faye. As she clears out her fridge to make room for the newly acquired food, she places a number of discarded items on a small table in the kitchen. At this point, she gestures over to the food caddy and suggests that "these things" are "great" and proceeds to explain that if she were to put discarded food in the normal kitchen bin, it would just be taken "to the dump;" but by placing it in the food caddy, it will be collected and go "to farmers" or put to use as compost. Notice the contrast between this and her interpretation of binning prior to the introduction of the food-recycling scheme as "game over." She jokes that she does not *actually* know what will happen to her discarded food because she did not read the information leaflet that they received at the same time as the bin, but the important point is that she anticipates and imagines that she is keeping food out of the waste stream by placing it in the caddy. She is therefore happy to manage her surplus and excess food in this way meaning that she and Chris have appropriated the device and incorporated it into their domestic food waste practices, and in a manner that is consistent with the intentions of the local authority.

The study reveals several reasons why households might respond less enthusiastically. For example, in one of my encounters with Tamsin we get on to the topic of food recycling and she confesses that she has never once used the bin that she was issued with, and that she has in fact stored it in the trunk of her car. Her reason for holding onto it is in case "they"—by which she means "the council"—ask for it back. Her reasons for not using it are multiple. For a start, her kitchen is relatively small and so she feels that she does not have the space to physically accommodate the recycling bin. Beyond this, she is bothered by the procedures that the device—especially in the context of the other receptacles that have already manifested themselves in her home—calls forth, such as separating materials, ensuring that they are placed in the correct bin and then making sure that the right bin is put out on the right day. It will be recalled that Tamsin's life is somewhat "hectic" and so even the apparently simple act of scheduling to put different bins out for collection is likely to be difficult, especially if she is liable to not be at home to take them out to the kerbside. A more subtle point (Bulkeley and Gregson 2009) relates to the ways in which food recycling bins represent an affront to interior aesthetics and kitchen design. Tamsin—in common with several other respondents—views them as "ugly," "garish," and *additional* "clutter" that is disruptive of "cleanliness and the display of order within home interiors" (Bulkeley and Gregson 2009: 937). She explicitly points out that she views her apartment as her "nest" and one that she tries to keep nice, meaning that she does not want a food recycling bin getting in the way of that. Additionally, when she first moved in she had to clean thoroughly in order to get rid of the "stink" that was left by the previous tenant, and so she is not willing to accept something that could make her home smell bad again.

Turning now to Wez who is divorced, in his mid fifties, and living in a large house on Leopold Lane; attention can be paid to the effects of food recycling schemes within certain neighborhoods (Bulkeley and Gregson 2009). In common with Tamsin, Wez is concerned with trying to keep things nice and considers food recycling a potential threat to cleanliness and order on Leopold Lane—however his worries reach beyond the borders of his own kitchen and home. He takes the view that most people make an effort to keep the street clean but is anxious that it would only take "one lot"—by which he is referring to an unruly group of (young) people—to decide that it would be "a laugh" to empty the bins when they are put out for collection, and then the food recycling scheme would lead to mess and problems. In addition to it looking unsightly, he suggests that this would undermine efforts to make the neighborhood "decent" and that food carries the added risk of attracting rats. In both of these examples, food recycling emerges as markedly different from "dry" recycling by virtue of its association with decaying, rotting, and unbecoming material. For Tamsin, if she were to miss the appropriate moment to put her food recycling bin out then it would offend the olfactory experience of being at home in ways that neglecting to put out "some glass and newspaper" would not. For Wez, the threat of "vermin" and the risk it poses to public health means that the problem is bigger than the mess that would be caused by "a few cans" being littered in the street insofar as the latter can be "more easily cleaned up."

Finally, it is important to remember that recycling bins are a very literal manifestation of waste management systems (Chappells and Shove 1999). As such, they have the potential to represent the creeping intrusions of "the council" into people's homes (Miller 1988; Bulkeley and Gregson 2009). Turning again to Wez, he in particular expresses resentment towards this and cites experiences earlier in his life when he lived in a "council flat"[7] and never felt that his home was his own, and that he always had to "play by their rules" or "run everything by them." Now that he owns his own home, he is unwilling to respond to invocations that require him to manage his kitchen in ways that are not of his choosing. This skepticism extends to his view of what the local authority will actually do with the material disposed of through the food caddy. In contrast to Faye's optimism that they will find a use for it, Wez suspects that it will probably just go to "the tip" anyway, and that it is nothing more than a PR exercise. Taking all of these points together, several respondents certainly do not appear willing to appropriate these devices as a means of managing the disposal of their surplus food. Crucially, it is the material presence of food caddies—and the representational effects that they generate—that prevent them from operating effectively as a conduit of disposal.

A more in-depth discussion of food waste bins based on sustained research can be drawn from the work of Alan Metcalfe and his colleagues (Metcalfe et al. 2013). They consider the material, representational and relational (Olsen 2010) aspects of food recycling bins and in common with the analysis above, suggest that it is their material agency that is most disruptive and troubling to households. Indeed, they suggest that issues of "smell, hygiene, size, aesthetics, order and respectability" (2013: 147) are of particular concern. However, their analysis goes further than mine in order to explore how households engage with, manage, and even accommodate the material agency and presence of the food caddy. At a general level, they suggest that although households may not like or may not want these devices in their home; they do not simply reject them and refuse to participate in food recycling schemes. To the contrary, they suggest that the material presence of the food caddy can actively enrol households and lead to changes in the ways that they manage the disposal of surplus and excess food. Additionally, they detail specific instances of households dealing with the polluting presence of the bin by developing cleaning and emptying routines, "making space" (2013: 141) for the caddy by locating it in areas (such as by the sink) already associated with dirt and disposal, and replacing the standard issue bin with a smaller receptacle.[8]

It is instructive to note that the household that utilized their own smaller receptacle made no objection—in contrast to Wez—to "the council" or the demands of the recycling scheme. Metcalfe et al. suggest that in fact "[t]he bin service was an extension of an idea that they already valued. It enabled what was waste to be reused for little effort on their part" (2013: 146). The only problem was with the specific material properties of the bin that had been supplied as part of the scheme. The difference between Wez's view and that of Metcalfe's respondent can be viewed as a reflection of the differences between the neighborhoods in which our respective studies took place. Their study took place in a "settled" and "middle class" area that is characterized by high recycling rates whereas mine did not. Metcalfe et al. (2013) nevertheless detail instances of households actively rejecting the presence of the food caddies and resisting the invocation to change their domestic waste practices. Taken together, two things are of particular significance: (1) that food-recycling bins are clearly ambiguous in their consequences *vis-à-vis* initiatives for waste reduction at the level of the household; and (2) that the material agency of objects (in this case, food-recycling bins) needs to be acknowledged in a phenomenological sense rather than simply looking through the material to seek agency in representational and relational registers (Olsen 2010; Metcalfe et al. 2013). This is certainly a useful way of thinking about food and its categorization as either "surplus" or "excess." These themes are now picked up for use in the next chapter, where I turn to a discussion of why alternative trajectories do not operate consistently or effectively to dispose of food in ways that keep it out of the waste stream.

–7–

Gifting, Re-use and Salvage

In theorizing the stabilization of the trajectories that connect surplus food to the waste stream, the previous chapter necessarily bypassed a detailed discussion of the multiple conduits that exist for "moving things along" (Gregson et al. 2007b). In stressing the overwhelming tendency for surplus and excess food to be placed in the bin, it was not my intention to deny the possibility of enacting its disposal differently. To the contrary, the development of an argument concerning the connections between surplus food and food waste requires that attention is paid to the workings (and shortcomings) of these alternative conduits. Accordingly, this chapter considers the ways in which surplus food can be re-circulated and redistributed, and so disposed of in ways that keep it from becoming excess and consequently routed through the waste stream. Additionally it considers the potential to recover excess matter, transform it, and save it from wastage by using it as something other than food. I suggest that none of these conduits operate consistently to effectively dispose of surplus and excess, less still to disrupt the transformation of "food" into "waste."

GIFTING

The re-circulation and re-distribution of surplus things via systems of gift exchange is well documented (various contributions to Schrift 1997). Students of anthropology will be familiar with Malinwoski's famous study of the Trobriand Islanders (1922) and his account of the yam harvest. The gifting and exchange of yams is said to make visible relationships of power, status, debt and obligation such that they are piled up outside of people's homes and left to rot. Traveling back to a contemporary U.K. context, it might reasonably be assumed that gifting could potentially provide a suitable conduit for disposing of surplus food in ways that save it from wastage. Indeed, Nicky Gregson and her colleagues are quite explicit in their suggestion that gifting is an effective mechanism for extending the social life of discarded consumer objects. For the residents of these ordinary streets in South Manchester, however, it would seem as if the gifting and exchange of food is fraught with anxiety and is therefore not a readily accessible nor commonly utilized conduit of disposal.

For example Andrew and Margaret are a retired couple who live in a three-bedroom house on Leopold Lane that they have shared for 29 years. During one of my first meetings with Andrew, he brings up the topic of sharing food with neighbors and reminisces fondly about an Indian family that used to live next door some 15 years previously, and who used to bring over the surplus of meals that had been prepared in their home for him to try. He and Margaret initially thought that this was a little odd because it is not something that they were used to, however they grew to really appreciate these gifts and Andrew in particular enjoyed being able to sample new things. Even so, they never reciprocated these gifts and at one level, Andrew suggests that this is because gifting food is not the "done thing." At another level, they are concerned about the food that they eat being "bland" or "boring"—especially by comparison. These anxieties around moving food along are echoed throughout the study. For a start, many of the households encountered do not pass along the surplus of meals that they have prepared in their homes because doing so would leave their culinary skills open to scrutiny by others. For example, when looking through the items in Sadie's fridge, we come to the leftovers of a pasta bake that she and her family had eaten the previous evening and she exclaims that she would be embarrassed by the thought of anybody else "sitting down" to eat it.

As far as Sadie is concerned, this meal is nothing special—it is a compromise between the imperative to cook "proper" food and the demands that are placed on her time during the week. So whilst she "cheats" a bit by using a stir-in sauce; she also uses good quality meat and lots of fresh vegetables to create a meal that is "healthy," "easy" and something that her family enjoy. Further, it is well understood that when people are cooking for others with whom they are not particularly close, they tend to cook more elaborate meals than they would when cooking for more immediate friends and family. This point is instructive for thinking about the recirculation of surplus food. Sadie is quite explicit in noting that when she cooks for people outside of her home, she wishes to appear as if she is a "domestic goddess" whereas her family accept that she is "not exactly Nigella."[1] Sadie is not at all embarrassed about serving the pasta bake to her family because it serves perfectly well as a mid-week meal.[2] However she considers it far too prosaic to be eaten by anybody outside of her home insofar as it does not showcase the effort and cooking skills that she would like others to associate with her kitchen practices.

At issue here is the potential for food to symbolize or to represent perceived culinary failings. In addition to not gifting the leftovers of meals that have been prepared and eaten, several households do not move along surplus in the form of unused ingredients. For example, on one occasion, Chris and Faye were sorting out their fridge ahead of going on holiday for a week, and they had spontaneously called me to invite me over as they thought that I might like to be there as they did so. At one point, Chris suggests that they should perhaps give some of the stuff that might go off to somebody in one of the other apartments in their block. In response, Faye picks up some processed cheese triangles in one hand, some low-cost supermarket own-brand sausages in the other and pulls a face of mock (I assume) incredulity and asks Chris if they really want to advertise their "scally buying"[3] to the world. Two things are of note here. Firstly, that even food that is "raw" in the sense of not being transformed or acted upon by households (Lévi-Strauss 1966) has the potential to symbolize and represent very private household arrangements. Secondly, that anxieties about opening up their taste in food to public scrutiny and the risk of being found "unsophisticated" works to prevent the gifting of "raw" surplus food. More generally it can be noted that these concerns around culinary competence and social respectability are manifest across most of the respondents, and that they appear to consistently reduce the likelihood of surplus food being re-circulated.

In addition to preventing or interrupting the flow of surplus foods that are feared to signify households falling short of desired standards, these same anxieties can also affect the trajectories of food that has the potential to demonstrate a degree of culinary competence or social respectability. For instance, on a different occasion I was doing a "cupboard rummage" with Faye and we started discussing a jar of artichoke hearts. She had purchased them because she felt that they are the kind of thing that you are supposed to get, and that she had seen them talked about on cookery shows and in lifestyle magazines. However, she also suspects that she will not use them because she does not know how to prepare them. The artichoke hearts are by now surplus to the requirements of her household consumption but they are by no means excess insofar as the jar has not been opened, they are well preserved (in olive oil) and are well within the limits of their "use by" date. Additionally, this is a desirable commodity with significant potential to be valued elsewhere and used by somebody else. However Faye fears that by moving them along, it would be equivalent to publically admitting that she does not possess the requisite culinary and cultural capital to consume the artichoke hearts.

Similarly, Julia suggests that she feels ashamed when she ends up buying fruit and vegetables and then not eating them because it makes her feel like one of "those women" who buy healthy things but end up "eating crap" instead. However in the context of one of her discussions about the guilt that she experiences when she throws food out, she confesses that she does not give these "perfectly good" surplus fruit and vegetables to her neighbors because she fears that upon receiving these gifts, they might read her as a "greedy fat cow" that doesn't eat properly or take care of her family. These examples illustrate how moving along so-called "good" foodstuffs is fraught with anxieties around the perceived social and culinary failings that are feared to be unveiled by doing so. Again, these concerns are manifest in several of the households and they appear to reduce the likelihood of good and symbolically valuable surplus food stuffs being productively disposed of through conduits of gift exchange.

Taken together, this suggests that food—especially surplus food—is a dangerous material and that its riskiness derives from its potential to stand for something else.[4] Chapter 4 demonstrated how surplus food represents a troubling reminder of "bad" household management and to this, it can be added that food is a material representation of domestic relationships and identities more generally. It follows that disposing of surplus food by gifting it—and so moving it beyond the threshold of the home—risks opening up these private attachments to public scrutiny. Whilst easy meals, unsophisticated tastes and the failure to cook or eat "good" ingredients are permissible within the relative security of the home; the households that participated in this study appear uneasy about releasing materials that would make these attachments and investments visible to anybody else. Returning now to the idea of food as an (un)becoming material, there is a sense in which the capacity for surplus to quickly and irrevocably become excess enables the cultural riskiness of food to be translated into more tangible concerns about its potential to make other people ill. In order for surplus food to comfortably pass from one household to another, it would first need to be divested of the meanings, associations and attachments that were fostered during processes of appropriation (see also Lucas 2002). However in the time taken for these traces of first-cycle consumption to be eradicated such that its social life might be extended, physical and microbial processes of self-transformation are liable to render surplus food unfit for consumption before it reaches the point at which it could be safely released without carrying forward the polluting effects of the excess. This conflation of physical and social "dirtiness" makes it much more likely that the offending material will be disposed of via the bin (see Chapter 6) as opposed to being re-circulated or disposed of through conduits of gift exchange.

It is not my intention to suggest that households cannot or do not dispose of surplus food by gifting it, however it is not a common occurrence amongst those that took part in this study. Further, the exceptional respondents and foodstuffs provide useful insights into why this might be the case. For example the majority of households appear comfortable with releasing tins, jars and packets of dry food from their homes in response to school and church campaigns to assemble harvest festival parcels for charitable purposes. This is entirely consistent with the analysis above insofar as households are able to gift these items anonymously (Cherrier 2009) and so bypass the risk of being scrutinized by the recipient. Similarly, Caroline's is the only household where surplus food moves in and out freely throughout the course of the study. It will be recalled from Chapter 5 that she lives very near, and is very close to, her daughter and daughter-in-law. To the extent that Caroline re-circulates surplus food by moving it beyond the threshold of her home, she does so through this well-established network of kin relations. Again, this is entirely consistent with the analysis above insofar as Caroline, her daughter, and her daughter-in-law are close enough to not have to worry about surplus food betraying their private and personal lives. Indeed, Caroline proudly tells me that they all view one another's houses as extensions of their own homes and throughout the study, I see this in action as her family frequently drop by unannounced and let themselves in using the keys that they have had cut. This fluid movement of surplus food (and indeed, individuals) is certainly not typical of the households encountered, suggesting that access to gifting as a conduit of disposal is shaped by contextual factors such as the extent to which persons are socially embedded within a locality.

I suspect that by now, several readers will be thinking about and recalling concrete instances in which they have given or received a gift of food. For example, the redistribution of allotment produce through gifting is a common-place occurrence in the U.K. (Crouch and Ward 1997) and beyond. However this is not the surplus of food that has been purchased for consumption, it is the surplus of food production and self-provisioning and so outside the remit of this book. Similarly, friends and colleagues very often regale me with stories of occasions in which they have shared food with their neighbors just as North American acquaintances are keen to remind me that the potluck is a persistent ritual in many silos of contemporary life. In response, I am minded to suggest that sharing food is not necessarily the same thing as gifting *surplus* in order to save it from wastage. More generally, I think it is fair to suggest that when people gift food, it tends to be things that they have baked (cakes, bread) or prepared especially (favorite recipes and "signature dishes"). In gifting these items, they are releasing something that they are comfortable with making visible—perhaps by virtue of the skill required to produce them.[5] Crucially, these items are a far cry from the surplus foodstuffs that are most at risk of going to waste, such as the afterwards of a prosaic weekday meal or half-used ingredients that might signify unsophisticated shopping habits.

Finally, when friends and colleagues report instances of gifting and sharing food, it is very often the case that they are either well embedded in a locality (as is the case with Caroline) or they live in a particular kind of neighborhood—one in which they (and others) are invested in various "community" and/or environmental issues. This underscores the point that households in the U.K. have differential access to gifting as a conduit of disposal.[6] In contrast, virtually everybody—at least in the U.K.—has unproblematic access to the public infrastructures that collect surplus and excess things for disposal into the waste stream. My argument, then, is that gifting—unlike binning—does not operate consistently as a means of disposing of surplus food, nor is it effective in disrupting its passage into waste. In contrast to the stability of the trajectories connecting surplus food to the waste stream, this conduit is characterized by shifting contours and gradients that reduce the possibilities of re-circulating surplus food by moving it between households. This instability, in part, might be attributed to the notable absence of material and infrastructural elements (bins, public systems of waste management). Additionally, I would suggest that the material, representational, and relational aspects of surplus food can be viewed as aligning not only to keep it out of this trajectory (gifting), but also to send it back in the direction of the waste stream via the bin.

RE-USE

Having discussed the difficulties associated with releasing surplus food from the home, it is important to now attend to its re-circulation *within* the home. There is good reason to expect that it might be less problematic given that Gregson et al. (2007a, 2007b) attest to the presence of hand-me-down economies operating within U.K. households (see also Clarke 2000) and that existing researches intimate that the activity of household food provisioning is premised on the gifting of food (DeVault 1991; Lupton 1996). The movement of surplus foodstuffs, however, follows a very different logic to those that do not—or have not yet become—surplus to requirements (see Cappellini 2009) and so "handing it down" appears not to be a commonly utilized conduit of disposal amongst the households encountered.

Part of the problem with surplus food is that it is not a suitable material through which to accomplish the work of feeding the family (see Chapters 3 and 4). For example, I was in Suzanne's kitchen one morning having arrived early for a shopping trip that we had arranged, and I am waiting (well, loitering) as she rushes around getting her children ready for school. Opening up the fridge to start making their packed lunches, she picks up a Tupperware container containing the leftovers from the previous night's meal and immediately dismisses it as a possibility. She proceeds to make their sandwiches and then adds a small box of raisins, a small packet of crisps, and a carton of juice to each of their lunchboxes. She explains that this is a combination that "they are into" but also one that she finds acceptable on the grounds that it is "reasonably healthy." Later on—as we are driving to the supermarket—I ask her about the leftovers that she rejected and she replies that she simply isn't willing to let them take cold pasta into school, and that she is concerned about how it would look—especially if the other children have "proper pack ups." This example provides a neat illustration of the aforementioned ideas around relations of care and devotion being materialized through the provision of food, and how this very often involves a balancing act between the preferences of the recipients and the imperative to eat properly.

Thinking now with Anne Allison's classic analysis (1991) of obentōs[7] and the manner in which the institution of the school nursery reproduces Japanese norms around food preparation and motherhood, this example also suggests that Suzanne might be anxious about releasing leftover food from her home because of what it might represent (see also Cappellini 2009). For example, it might expose her children as unusual amongst their peers at school or it might signify poor parenting on her part. However, Suzanne's interactions with leftovers elsewhere in the study help in contextualizing this observation, and in making a slightly more subtle point. For example, on another occasion I was in Suzanne's kitchen as she sets about the task of cooking an evening meal for her children, who will need to eat something other than the chicken breast and steamed vegetables that she is preparing for herself. Looking through the fridge, she picks up a Tupperware box that contains some leftover sausage casserole from the previous evening and explains that she will definitely not be giving this to her children for the second night in a row. She considers it "lazy" and "boring" to repeat meals and suggests that cooking something "quick" and "from the freezer" is a better option. Whilst re-heating some leftovers is quite probably no more "lazy" or "boring" than heating up some freezer food, Suzanne anticipates that her children will perceive one as "new" and the other as "old." More to the point, this distinction matters profoundly to her and it suggests that the continued materialization of love and devotion requires food to be prepared anew instead of simply giving what is there and ready to hand. By the time "food" becomes "surplus," its potential to express and constitute familial relations of love and devotion appears diminished insofar as it is "polluted" by the trace of first-cycle consumption. Crucially, the leftover sausage casserole is eventually placed in the bin, meaning that the option of feeding it to her children was not available or effective as a conduit through which to enact the disposal of this surplus food.

One of the reasons for this is that children are increasingly eating different meals to the adults in the household. In addition to fuelling the over provisioning of food (see Chapter 4), this trend also means that the surplus of adult food consumption is unlikely to be disposed of in ways that carry it onto children's dinner plates or into their lunchboxes. This idea can be developed in order to encompass a discussion of the ways in which people feed their pets. In the households that I studied, domestic animals are fed specialized and separate meals to the humans that they live with. Again, the provision of these foods can be viewed as a mechanism through which people materialize and express relations of care and devotion to their loved ones—including their pets. For example, on one occasion I was in the pet food aisle of a large supermarket during a shopping trip with Natalie. She picks up some branded cat food but before putting it into her trolley, realizes that it is the wrong one because her cat prefers his meat in jelly to meat in gravy. She explains that his favorite brand is too expensive to purchase all of the time, although she does get it for him at Christmas. Turning to the dried varieties of cat food on the shelves, she points out that she would never buy these, even though they are cheaper and her cat really likes them, because she does not think that they are good for his health—especially as he gets older and less active. Looking at the staggering variety of cat food products, Natalie discusses how her cat is very fussy and will not eat certain brands, especially not the supermarket's own brand, and as such, she will not purchase any of these. Her solution is to go for a "mid-range" product that she knows he likes and that she deems "good for him," but is not too expensive.

The care that Natalie puts into selecting just the right food for her cat provides an illustration and extension of Miller's argument (2001b) that our relationships with things can actually be expressive and constitutive of our relationships with others—in this case, with animals. It also demonstrates how important her cat is to her and provides a clue as to why she does not use the surplus of human food consumption as a means of feeding him. It is commonly held that surplus food used to be given to animals (see Strasser, 1999) and so it follows that the practice of expressing love and devotion towards animals through the provision of dedicated and specifically manufactured pet food is a relatively recent phenomenon. There is most likely a fascinating history of human-animal relations and the political economy of pet food that is yet to be written, however that is beyond the scope of this short book. The important point for now is that this development results in domestic animals—as is the case with children—no longer operating consistently as an effective conduit through which to dispose of surplus food and disrupt its passage into waste. This can be interpreted as increasing specialization in consumption (Shove and Warde 2002) stemming both from the diversification of products (pet food, food for children) and prevailing cultural conventions that equate competence (in food practices, parenting, and animal ownership) with consuming in certain ways rather than others (see Warde 2005). Taken together, the differences between humans and animals—or adults and children—are reflected in the infrastructural provision of different foodstuffs, and their appropriation and use by households (see James et al. 2009).

As was the case with my discussion of gifting and releasing surplus food from the home, I am not suggesting that households *never* dispose of surplus food by handing it down. For example in their analysis of consuming leftovers, Benedetta Cappellini and Elizabeth Parsons (2013) demonstrate how the re-use of surplus food can be occasioned by a collective sacrifice that involves all members of the household (including children) and that participation in this ritual marks and reinforces their belonging to the family unit. My study supports Cappellini and Parsons' analysis, however, the important point here is that the collective consumption of leftovers does not happen as a matter of course, rather it is more likely to take place on a Saturday afternoon when all members of the household are around and have the time to participate. Either way, children are not routinely and consistently fed surplus food (especially in the absence of other family members to share in the sacrifice) because doing so as a matter of course is understood as tantamount to not caring. Similarly, the respondents certainly do feed the afterwards of food consumption to their pets—a bit of hard cheese for the cat who mysteriously appears whilst a sandwich is being made or the fat from a pork chop for the dog that has been waiting patiently throughout the meal. However these gifts are seen as treats, snacks or supplements to the animal's core diet of pet food. So without disputing that households can be very creative in finding ways to extend the social life of surplus food; my argument is that its re-circulation within the home is problematic. In common with the trajectories through which it might be released from the home, these conduits are characterized by shifting contours and gradients such that they may not operate consistently or effectively to enact the disposal of surplus food, nor to save it from wastage.

SALVAGE

The preceding analysis addressed the conduits available for the disposal of *surplus* food—stuff that people have decided they do not need or want, but that could have still conceivably been used to feed somebody or something (in the case of pets) else. This section considers the potential to recover excess—non-food—and so prevent its final transformation into waste. The vitality of (once) edible matter and its potential for self-transformation means that even when it is no longer food, it might still be useful in some other capacity. Indeed, if excess is placed in conduits that enable it to be converted into compost, then it might productively be disposed of.[8] Despite this potential, the fieldwork suggests that it might be a tricky maneuver. For a start, many respondents view home composting as an activity that people "like them" do not do. For example, Natalie has a colleague who works at a high-end salon in an affluent area just outside of Manchester, and suggests that only people "like her"—who live in the countryside and are "all nuts and berries" (see Evans 2012b)—are invested in such things. Others position home composting as something that they might like to do but are limited by the physical dimensions and layout of their home. For example, Nikki is in her early thirties and lives with her boyfriend in a one-bedroom flat on Leopold Lane. Early on in the study—before the food-recycling scheme was introduced—I was sat in her apartment discussing the things that she would like to do in order to reduce the amount of food that they waste. She brings up composting as a possibility but quickly dismisses it on the grounds that it wouldn't really work for her. Gesturing at me to look around her kitchen, she points out that she has limited space, much of which is already taken up by boxes and bags for rubbish and recycling. She concludes that she does not have the room to set up another receptacle for collecting compostable matter, and that she would not be prepared to do something that would make her flat smell bad. Note how these concerns anticipate some of the objections that were later made in response to the introduction of food caddies (see Chapter 6).

One of the most powerful examples of home composting refusing to dispose of excess or divert it from the waste stream can be drawn from the experiences of Rachel and Paul—a school teacher and a trainee social worker, both in their mid twenties, who rent a two-bedroom terraced house on Rosewall Crescent. Rachel and Paul are invested and interested in "green" issues and as part of this, they were initially keen and optimistic about using their discarded food to produce compost. Indeed, they both thought that it was a really good idea on the grounds that it would find a use for stuff that would otherwise go to waste. However, their attempts at composting were fraught with problems. For a start, they soon realized that discarded food is not sufficient in isolation to make good compost and having been told that "green waste" was the missing ingredient, they faced the reality that they do not have access to this. In common with much of the housing stock in Manchester, they have a back yard and not a garden, and although they have several pot plants and grow-bags; this does not generate enough "garden waste" to help them make usable compost.

Paul suggests that they could perhaps do more with their outside space in order to address this but notes that neither he nor Rachel are "into gardening" and speculates that it is something that older people do, or people with more time on their hands. This links the second major problem that they encountered: namely that they do not have much use for compost. Rachel points out that they were "composting for the sake of composting" and reports "asking around" to see if anybody might have a use for the results of their efforts but quickly realized that people who lived in a similar house to theirs had no need for compost and found it odd to have been asked. People with a garden were either able to make their own or would reject the poor-quality compost that Paul and Rachel are able to produce. In the end, their efforts to translate the residual value of excess food were unsuccessful and the resultant matter was placed in the bin. Again this is not to dispute that households can and do utilize home composting as a means of enacting the disposal of discarded food, it is simply to highlight its instability and some of the disparities in access to it.

In addition to attempts at recovering excess via its wholesale transformation, it is also conceivable that matter that is becoming excess might undergo a more modest transformation in order to be salvaged and used as food. Chapter 5 illustrated how food that is "on the turn" but still safe to eat might be recovered from the gap in disposal to realize a use in ways that mask its decline in taste or quality (for example by stirring it into a curry sauce). Similarly, I witnessed several households cut out mould in order to prevent it from contaminating a whole block of cheese. In contrast, I was once going through the items in Wez's fridge and he picks up some potato cakes—there are four left in a pack of six, two with bits of mould on them—and puts them straight in the bin. He explains that the presence of the mould means that there is no chance of him eating them, and that where he had witnessed his grandparents picking the mould off bread and then toasting it; he does not consider himself so "hard up" that he should have to eat mouldy food. Elsewhere in the study, he describes himself as having "come good" from a relatively impoverished background and so being in a position where he is able to dispose of food emerges as important to his narrative of social mobility and respectability. This example illustrates that it is not always relations of love and devotion that prevent the re-use of food insofar as issues of self-identity and perceptions of the alignment between handling dirty things and residual social categories (see also Reno 2009) are also coming into play.

It will be recalled that food that is left over after people have eaten (such as food left on the plate after the meal) tends to go straight into the bin rather than entering the gap in disposal. Curiously, these foodstuffs are almost always likely to be safe to eat but their representational effects are so severe, so polluting, that they are hard to imagine as anything other than excess. For example, George is a marketing manager in his early forties who lives on Leopold Lane with his partner and their three young children. On one occasion, George and I were sitting in a pub having decided to go for a drink after completing a "formal" interview in his home. A group of friends are dining at a table near to where we are sat and when they leave, we notice that there is a considerable amount of food left on almost all of their plates. George points out that he considers this a real waste of food and muses out loud that it is odd that most of us would find it inappropriate—disgusting even—to go and eat these leftovers. He then recalls how he had recently eaten half a hot dog that his daughter had left on her plate during a barbeque he and his partner had organized in order to celebrate a family birthday. It turns out that he had not had chance to eat as he was too busy barbequing the food for everybody else, and by the time he got around to sorting himself out, there was no meat left and he was "starving." He explains how there were lots of half finished hotdogs and burgers that he wasn't prepared to eat because they had belonged to "other people's children," and so he had to wait patiently for a member of his family to leave something.

George is quick to point out that he would not normally eat food that one of his children has left on their plate because, quite simply, he would not have to. When he and his family eat together, he normally has enough food of his own and would consider it gluttonous to then eat surplus food that he does not want or need. This of course speaks to a more general question about when or if eating beyond an efficient calorific intake ceases to be an effective strategy for productively managing the disposal of surplus food and becomes wasteful in and of itself. Suffice to say, the respondents were found to be managing and negotiating this issue in a number of different ways. Several appear to engage in the modern practice of displaying dietary and bodily restraint by deliberately not eating all that is made available for their consumption whereas others seem to make a virtue out of cleaning their plate. George captures these issues most succinctly when he explains how his metabolism has slowed down now that he has started to get older. Consequently, his youthful commitment to "not wasting food" has given way to a middle-aged concern with "not letting his waist expand." The connections between overconsumption and obesity are, quite frankly, too big to do justice to within the confines of this book or in the context of my discussions around surplus, disposal and food waste.[9]

The key point to be taken from the analysis in this chapter is that in contrast to the bin; placing surplus food (or excess) in any of these alternative conduits will not consistently lead to their effective disposal. Similarly, they cannot be relied upon to enact its disposal in ways that save it from wastage. They are characterized by shifting social and semiotic gradients, and this instability helps to explain why binning remains normative and the appropriate conduit through which to manage the disposal of surplus food.

–8–

Conclusion: Living with Food, Reducing Waste

In summary, this book has gone behind closed doors—into the lives and homes of ordinary people—to explore some of the ways in which stuff that is "food" becomes stuff that is "waste." Chapters 3 and 4 focussed on how "food" becomes "surplus" and the gist of the argument developed here is that these movements have become normalized through the collective development of interlocking practices such that surplus is now embedded in the flow of everyday life. Chapter 5 considered what happens to surplus food and found that whatever households eventually do with it, their first step is to place it in a "gap." The analysis suggests that a lot can happen once this gap is opened up, and that it is by no means a black hole into which surplus food irreversibly disappears. However it was argued that that "surplus" overwhelmingly exits the gap as "excess" whereupon it gets placed in conduits that connect it to the waste stream. In order to make sense of this, Chapters 6 and 7 paid attention to the workings of different conduits of disposal. Here it was argued that in contrast to the stability of the trajectories that connect surplus food to the waste stream; alternative conduits do not operate consistently to effectively dispose of surplus and excess food, nor do they do so in ways that save it from wastage. Bringing these insights together, this concluding chapter begins by taking the opportunity to sharpen the concepts and clarify the vocabulary that we as social scientists use as we begin to flesh out our understandings of household food waste. With this in place I develop a discrete argument and my own theoretical position that will then segue into a discussion of what the account put forward here might mean in relation to policies and practical initiatives for food waste reduction.

INGREDIENTS FOR A SOCIOLOGICAL THEORY OF HOUSEHOLD FOOD WASTE

Before extrapolating from this analysis to offer a framework for thinking about household food waste, it is important to acknowledge that I am drawing principally on a small-scale ethnographic study of urban households in a specific region of the U.K. As such, I make no claims to representativeness or generalizability. Nevertheless, this research represents an important first step in addressing the issue of food waste in a manner that is attuned to contemporary social science perspectives on home consumption, material culture and everyday life. Further, the empirical material and my analysis of it provides the basis for a theoretical *sketch* to be populated by additional perspectives and further researches. Indeed, by exploring the processes and practices that accompany the passage of "food" into "waste," it transpires that there are a number of movements and steps that need to be understood, and that future studies might productively explore these. As such, my sketch (figure 1) is intended as programmatic rather than definitive:

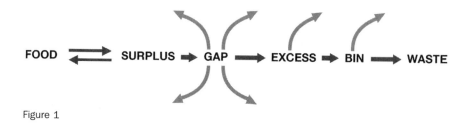

Figure 1

The first thing to note is that this diagram implies that "food" follows a linear progression *en route* to becoming "waste." This is not a tacit endorsement of unidirectional thinking or modeling; it is a reflection of the fact that rather a lot of food (both in this study and in households more generally) ends up as waste. That being so, it is worth trying to make sense of why this is happening. At its core, this sketch suggests that it is important to separate out the concepts of "surplus," "excess," and "waste." These concepts are often confused and used interchangeably but the analysis here suggests that the terms "surplus" and "excess" pertain to very different categories of object, and that the term "waste" refers to the placing of these objects. In this view, "waste" is not something to be disposed of; it is a consequence of how something is disposed of. By extension, this implies that efforts to conceptualize household food waste could usefully focus on tracing the ways in which "food" becomes "surplus," and how this in turn becomes "excess" and then "waste."

Figure 1 also suggests that this process is punctuated by a "gap", and the curved arrows represent the multiple conduits in which surplus foodstuffs might be placed and consequently disposed of. The arrows are curved in order to reflect the shifting gradients and contours of these conduits, and the uncertainties surrounding the direction in which they will route surplus things once they have been released from the gap. The curved arrow associated with "excess" represents another conduit of disposal, specifically the potential to recover things that households have deemed unfit for consumption as food by transforming them and using them as something else. It also signals that even if a given household has categorized something as "non-food"; others—such as dumpster divers—may beg to differ. One man's (sic) trash, as the old adage goes, is another's treasure. Bins occupy a central location in this sketch insofar as they operate consistently and effectively to connect surplus and excess things to the waste stream. The curved arrow here acknowledges that even stuff that has been placed in a bin—for example, a food recycling caddy—can still be disposed of in ways that keep it out of the waste stream.

I wish to suggest that the sketch above (figure 1) is a useful framework around which to organize and position future studies of household food waste. Indeed, my account is necessarily specific to my empirical material and as such, there is a lot more work to be done in order to fill in the gaps. For example, it would be useful to know how and why (or even if) "food" becomes "surplus" in different national contexts, where the patterning of everyday life and infrastructures of grocery shopping are completely different to those reported above. Similarly, it would be useful to empirically capture instances in which alternative conduits operate more consistently and effectively to dispose of surplus food, and to save it from wastage. From a slightly different angle, it would be worth exploring the different regulatory regimes in which food-recycling schemes have been introduced more successfully than is currently the case in the U.K. As noted, the burgeoning body of work on dumpster diving (for example Edwards and Mercer 2013) can be plotted against the conduits of disposal associated with "excess" and the bin, but to this I might add (following O'Brien 2013) that questions of who owns garbage—especially as it crosses the public/private divide—are a potentially fruitful avenue for further research. More generally, it is necessary to explore the ways in which these issues cut across the lines of class, ethnicity, age and place. No matter how "ordinary" the participants in my own study are, I would expect a good deal of variation across households in different socio-economic positions (whilst my respondents are heterogeneous, the group are skewed towards lower-middle class families and young professionals), ethnic and religious background (the majority of my respondents are white and nominally Christian), and geography (for example, my respondents reflect an "urban" experience of food waste and this is likely to be very different in rural areas).

Returning now to my own analysis and the development of a discrete argument, this sketch can now be overlaid with a number of other items (figure 2):

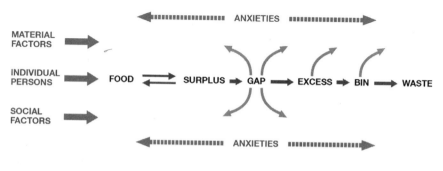

Figure 2

Throughout this book, I have advocated approaches that move beyond a narrow and restrictive focus on the individuals who can ostensibly be viewed as occasioning and enacting the various movements through which "food" becomes "waste." To this effect, figure 2 attempts to capture the contextual factors that provide the backdrop to these performances. For ease of practical representation, I have categorized some of these as "material" and others as "social" but I wish to emphasize that on an intellectual level, I consider it inappropriate and deeply problematic to make such an artificial distinction. My argument, then, is that some of these contextual factors can be thought of as non-human (for example bins, domestic technologies, food packaging, and microbial life) whereas others are "social"[1] in the sense that they extend beyond individual persons (for example tastes, conventions, time, and relationships with significant others). The diagram also signals that multiple anxieties are present, and that they accompany the processes through which "food" becomes "waste." At this juncture, it is important to pause and bring together a number of empirical themes with contemporary theoretical perspectives in order to think about anxiety in more detail.

ANXIETY

Recent work by Peter Jackson and his colleagues (for example Jackson and Everts 2010; Milne et al. 2011; Meah and Watson 2012; Watson and Meah 2012; Jackson et al. 2013) has put forward an approach to anxiety that moves beyond conceptualizing it as a personality disorder, or as the sole preserve of individuals, in order to address its presence and location "in the social" (Jackson et al. 2013). They draw upon a range of social theorists and philosophers ranging from Heidegger and Kierkegaard to Deleuze and Badiou, however two sources of inspiration are particularly noteworthy. First, they build on Iain Wilkinson's claim that anxieties can usefully be understood as the "consequence of the social predicaments and cultural contradictions in which individuals are made to live out their everyday lives" (Wilkinson 2001: 17). Second, they very explicitly align their account of anxiety with theories of practice (see Chapter 2) to suggest that:

> [A]nxiety is not some free-floating mental activity; it is embodied in specific (often complex) doings and sayings. Anxieties are embodied and social, practical and practised. Like other social practices, they are routinized, collective, and conventional in character (Jackson and Everts 2011: 2801)

In addition to being theoretically significant in and of itself, they apply this analysis to consumer anxieties about food and as such, it is particularly relevant to the arguments at hand.

In suggesting that anxieties accompany the processes through which food becomes waste, I mean several things. At a basic level, I am suggesting that households are anxious about the food that they waste, however I am also suggesting that they are concomitantly negotiating a range of complex and contradictory anxieties. These include concerns about food safety, food provenance, healthy eating, eating "properly," and calorific intake. Many of these play a role in directing food towards the waste stream. Additionally, I am suggesting that these food-related anxieties are caught up with, and spill over into, a range of other concerns (see Jackson et al. 2013). For example, I have illustrated how anxieties around food connect to concerns about how best to care for the self and significant others, as well as to questions of class, identity and social respectability. Again, these anxieties have been shown to shape the processes through which "food" becomes "waste."

Does this mean, then, that households are perpetually in a state of psychological and physiological anxiety? No, of course not, and it is important to clarify that the absence of empirically observable anxieties does not necessarily mean that they do not have—or have not had—any bearing on the trajectories of the practices that currently constitute the patterning of everyday life. According to Peter Jackson and his colleagues, anxieties are social forces that become routinized and institutionalized in collective patterns and practices of consumption. They suggest that the circulation of particular food-related anxieties (such as those surrounding the spread of avian influenza) have the potential to disrupt the existing flow of everyday life, at which point they can be experienced subjectively—in the psychological and physiological sense of feeling anxious. However, the strategies and tactics developed in response to these shocks soon become part of the reconfigured practices that households go on to undertake without too much in way of conscious and deliberate reflection. Effectively, anxieties are displaced and incorporated into routine activities. For example the overwhelming tendency for households to hold onto surplus food rather than immediately placing it in the bin can be interpreted as a normal and appropriate way of doing things, and one that results from anxieties about wasting food being collectively negotiated into domestic practices—and mediated by household technologies such as refrigerators and Tupperware containers—over time.

Without disputing that individual embodied subjects are the site at which anxieties are subjectively experienced, they suggest that this is a relationally constituted moment that has origins and consequences across a range of actors, and at a variety of scales. In order to account for the presence of phenomena that are not guaranteed to be tangible, they suggest an analytic strategy of "tracing" the contours of anxieties "as they are mediated and circulate within society" (Jackson et al. 2013). This invites a focus both on how (and by whom) anxieties are framed, represented and transmitted, and on the actions taken (consumer responses but also legislative and regulatory measures) in response to an anxiety taking hold. Of particular note are claims that social anxieties give rise to a moralizing agenda and that currently, there appears to be an appetite for campaigns that deliberately seek to heighten levels of public anxiety (Jackson and Everts 2010; Watson and Meah 2013). It is not difficult to identify the circulation of anxieties around food waste, or to see how they moralize acts of waste reduction (see also Chapters 1 and 2). Indeed a range of actors ranging from policy makers and third sector organizations to food retailers and celebrity chefs are currently involved, perhaps inadvertently, in efforts that appear to be adding to the stock of food-related anxieties, especially around waste. These range from the very visual (e.g. images of vast quantities of rotting food), through the rhetoric of scandal and crisis, to facts and figures (contextualized to be of the utmost relevance to households) concerning the financial costs of wasting food. Similarly, at the time of writing, U.K. celebrity chef Jamie Oliver is under scrutiny for attempting to tackle food waste in a manner that has offended a number of sensitivities around class and regional identities.

Leaving aside arguments that this approach might lead to alienation or compassion fatigue (see Hawkins 2006), it is important to recognize that this sort of affective communication with households and consumers may not have the desired effects. As Richard Milne and his colleagues point out, these strategies *"activate* rather than *direct* affective bodies, with unpredictable effects"* (Milne et al. 2011: 185). This means that as consumers subjectively experience a moment of social anxiety that disrupts their existing routines, there are no guarantees that practices will be individually or collectively re-configured in a manner that will yield the desired and intended consequences. Indeed, as Chapter 4 made clear—in its analysis of thrift, anxiety, and waste generation—these efforts may even have the opposite effect. This brings the discussion back to the more general point that current approaches to food waste reduction are sub-optimal. In making this claim, it is important that I make some effort to propose an alternative. It is to this issue that I now turn.

WASTE REDUCTION

It is not my intention to offer concrete recommendations for food waste reduction, rather the emphasis here is on thinking about how debates in waste policy and research might be re-orientated in light of social science perspectives on home consumption, material culture, and everyday life. My first step is to summarize a number of arguments that cut across the insights above, and are potentially relevant if the policy goal is to reduce food waste. The first is that "food" becomes "waste" through a complex and anxiety-laden process (see also Gregson et al. 2007a). This means that the tangible and quantifiable act of binning should not be taken as evidence of households not caring about the food that they waste. It also means that there is a lot going on "behind the scenes" to give rise to this troublesome end point. Allied to this, my second argument is that the behaviors that give rise to waste are not necessarily waste-related. As counterintuitive as this may seem, the point I am making is that when households put food in the bin it has very little to do with their attitudes and orientations towards waste or the environment. Efforts that seek to change this behavior are liable to miss the ways in which "waste" is a consequence of other—often unrelated—things. I have already illustrated that food waste can be interpreted in relation to a number of different factors ranging from people feeling compelled to purchase particular types of food, through caring for significant others, to the various demands that are placed on household schedules. More importantly, I have argued that food waste can be understood as the fallout of the ways in which these things—and more besides—intersect, overlap, and are negotiated by households. Viewed as such, efforts to reduce food waste might usefully be targeted at behaviors that appear not to have anything much to do with waste. For example, it seems reasonable to think that efforts to change the ways in which households acquire food might have the knock-on effect of reducing food waste without ever having to target "waste behaviors" directly. Similarly, it is not inconceivable that efforts to change other practices—for example those that relate to mobility, housing, caring and dwelling—might have similar ramifications in terms of engendering food waste reduction.

My third argument is one that has already been made by Catherine Alexander and her colleagues, namely that "not all wastage *in* households is caused *by* the individual consumer" (Alexander et al. 2013). The point here is that the causes of household food waste can actually occur earlier in the food chain meaning that responsibilities for dealing with it should not be restricted to the locations in which it arises. The best illustration of this are the retail practices (and those of the food industry more generally) that pass the burden of surplus on to households by, for example, making food available in excessive quantities.[2] Taking these three points together, my suggestion is that policies for waste reduction should focus on the various factors (economic, political, material, institutional, social, and cultural) that shape patterns of food consumption, the organization of everyday life and the trajectories through which things can be moved along. The discussion that follows is a series of ideas that follow logically from my account of why households waste food in the first place. I make no claims as to the novelty or feasibility of these suggestions, and would urge that they are interpreted as a series of thought experiments designed to consider the mechanisms and approaches that are consistent with my theoretical position on household food waste.

Policies for waste reduction can be plotted against the broad categories of waste prevention and waste diversion (Bulkeley et al. 2007). In the language of my theoretical sketch, it follows that initiatives to reduce household food waste can either take the form of efforts to *prevent* the acquisition of surplus food, or efforts to *divert* it from the waste stream. The most significant environmental and social gains are likely to come from policies that successfully prevent food from ever becoming surplus. Indeed there are greenhouse gas emissions embedded in the production of food that is surplus to requirements, and this is problematic—even if the surplus is successfully diverted from the waste stream.[3] Efforts to prevent the production and acquisition of surplus food are, however, liable to be thwarted by a degree of structural lock-in and systemic inertia. Conversely, initiatives that seek to divert surplus from the waste stream are perhaps more likely to succeed, but with effects that are less significant. Viewed as such, it makes sense for waste policy to pursue a combination of waste prevention and waste diversion strategies.[4]

In terms of thinking about the reasons why "food" becomes "surplus," two of the clearest points to come out of this research are that: (1) shared understandings and definitions of what it means to eat "properly" help to create the conditions in which food is at risk of wastage; and (2) that food—especially "proper" food—is currently made available in quantities that exceed those that households are able to keep on top of. One possible inter-vention that follows from these insights relates to the ways in which the food industry makes fresh vegetables available for acquisition by households. My suggestion, then, is to promote the purchase of pre-made packets of mixed vegetables[5] that might allow households to cook "proper" meals without having to acquire a surplus of perishable ingredients that are liable to end up as waste. If the vegetables are already prepared, then they might relieve some of the time pressures that confront households as well as having the added benefit of bringing aesthetically imperfect produce onto supermarket shelves (thus preventing waste earlier on in the food chain). A potential issue is that the purchase and use of these vegetable packets is liable to be seen as "cheating," and so there would need to be a shift in shared under-standings and definitions of proper food.

It is not easy to design initiatives that will successfully bring about changes in these collective conventions, but it seems sensible to assume a number of different actors will have a role to play. For example, food retailers (and their suppliers) would need to collaborate in order to ensure that suitable products are made available. Packets of mixed vegetables are already available for purchase, but—in the U.K. at least—they tend not to cover the variety of different dishes that households want to eat. For example, my local supermarket stocks "stew packs," but this initiative would require that similar "packs" are made available to aid in the preparation of Thai curries, stir fries, Italian dishes, and so on. Food retailers could promote these packets alongside complementary products such as stir-in sauces, herb/spice mixes or tinned tomatoes in order to signal that these go well together. There is also a role for cultural intermediaries such as celebrity chefs who are well placed to circulate different ideas about what it means to cook and eat properly. For example, if these packets of mixed vegetables were to be promoted alongside recipe cards endorsed by credible chefs and a campaign that positions their use as "proper cooking" for "modern" or "busy" lives, then the idea that it is okay to "cheat" might start to take hold. Additionally, NGOs and third sector advocates could lend support and kudos to any such campaign. This is of course a very specific example, but it is intended as an invitation to think about portion sizes, shared definitions of proper food, the relationship between the different factors that give rise to waste, and the role of different actors and organizations in facilitating change.

Another—perhaps more radical—approach might be to think about how, where, and when meals are eaten. In the U.K., it is commonplace to eat the "main meal" of the day in the evening, and for this meal to be provisioned and consumed in private households. If this convention were to shift such that people eat their main meals in the middle of the day, and that these meals are provisioned and consumed outside of the home, then some of the pressures that are currently placed on individuals (time, conflicting social anxieties) might be alleviated. Additionally, it might cut down on the routine overprovisioning of perishable food that private households then struggle to find a use for. It doesn't take too much imagination to realize that this shift would be difficult to engender, however it is not inconceivable that measures to subsidize workplace canteens or school lunches might help in doing so. Indeed, discussions are already underway in Finland about adopting this as an approach to promoting healthier patterns of eating. This sort of initiative would require a sustained effort by central government as well as the participation of employers and other public institutions such as schools and day care centres. It would also require that people respond positively to these initiatives in suitable numbers, and with sufficient regularity for the shift to be significant and durable enough to have tangible consequences in terms of food waste prevention.

It is by no means a foregone conclusion that citizens will collectively respond to this initiative in the ways that might be hoped for, and part of the problem relates to the existing landscape in which it would have to take hold. For example in a culture where notions of eating as a family and eating in the home are deeply entrenched and bestowed with high levels of symbolic value, it is likely that measures that threaten these cherished ideals will be met with resistance. Perhaps, then, there is a role for programmatic measures that first address some of these potential sticking points before attempting to introduce the initiative under consideration. For example, one might argue that the success of the recent ban on smoking in public places in the U.K. is result of the various measures that preceded it (such as public health campaigns, taxation, and legislation) and that it might not have gone so smoothly had these measures not already been in place. By extension, this implies an even more significant role for governments in terms of setting an agenda, co-ordinating different actors and providing financial backing for an emerging suite of measures (Evans et al. 2012).

Turning now to initiatives that seek to divert surplus food from the waste stream, it becomes immediately apparent that this is currently the preferred policy response. As discussed in Chapter 6, food-recycling schemes appear—at first glance—consistent with the account of household food waste that has been developed here. However, I have also suggested that households may not readily adopt these devices or appropriate them into their domestic food waste practices. In their analysis of food recycling bins, Metcalfe et al. (2013) respond to a similar suite of problems by suggesting:

> One solution would be to offer different caddies, by size, shape and colour [...] injecting some flexibility into the material agency of the bin [...] would be a way of allowing people some control over troublesome issues (Metcalfe et al. 2013: 147)

I fully support this suggestion and to it, I would add that it is worth thinking about measures that provide shared facilities for food recycling, and to locate them outside of private households. For example, if people were to only have a very small food caddy in their kitchen (as per Alan Metcalfe's suggestions) coupled with the ability to frequently place their food recycling outside of their home whenever they wish, then many of the issues associated with space, scheduling, domestic aesthetics and "ickiness" (Metcalfe et al. 2013) might be overcome. Similarly, shared spaces for neighborhood-composting schemes—perhaps in tandem with community garden initiatives—might overcome some of the difficulties (not wanting to, not being able to, having no use for) associated with home composting.

At this juncture it is important to signal the potential risks of successfully managing to divert surplus and excess food from the waste stream. If households are able to manage their surplus food by composting or recycling it; they may well feel as if they have dealt sufficiently with the problem of food waste. In turn, this might mean that no further measures will be taken to tackle the routine acquisition of surplus food. The same might be true of the various scales at which waste policies are made. For example, a regime in which surplus and excess food is fed into anaerobic digesters and turned into energy is likely to be viewed as one that is dealing effectively with food waste—and for good reason. However there is a chance that this will obviate the need to take action on preventing the production and acquisition of surplus food. Further, it could well create a situation in which households are incentivized to produce more surplus food in order to supply the demands of the anaerobic digestion plant. Whilst these measures are of course preferable to food going to landfill, they might re-enforce an approach to waste policy that focuses on the least favored options within the waste hierarchy.

The preceding analysis has argued that surplus food ends up in the kitchen bin because alternative conduits and trajectories do not operate consistently to effectively dispose of it or to save it from wastage. One of the clearest indications of this relates to the ways in which people are anxious about releasing surplus food from the home by virtue of the identities and relations that would be made visible by doing so. In Chapter 7, it was argued that households appear to be more comfortable with gifting surplus food when they can do so in ways that shield them from the risk of being scrutinized by the recipient. The challenge for the policy makers, then, might be to develop mechanisms through which households can re-circulate surplus food but remain anonymous. There are already organizations—for example FareShare and Foodcycle in the U.K.—that take surplus (and so still "fit for purpose") produce from businesses and then redirect it in order to feed vulnerable groups. If there was a way to extend this scheme to collect and re-distribute surplus food from people's homes, then it might provide a suitable conduit through which to divert it from the waste stream. From a slightly different angle, there are emerging niches in which people are utilizing Smartphone technologies that enable them to locate and eat other people's surplus food. Whether or not this development will eventually operate consistently and effectively across all foodstuffs and across different groups of people remains to be seen. However, in addition to signalling the possibilities of "swapping leftovers," it also represents the nascent murmurings of a move— no matter how small or marginal—towards the collective provisioning of food. In turn, these might herald a potential solution to the problem of surplus production and acquisition.

Chapter 7 also argued that surplus food might circulate more freely between households when there are more tangible and meaningful connections between the persons that occupy different dwelling structures. Without wishing to sound glib, this implies a role for interventions that strengthen social ties and bonds within particular localities or neighborhoods. To be more constructive—albeit on the basis of a personal anecdote—the design and development of future housing might provide a useful entry point here. For example, between the time of doing the fieldwork and sitting down to write this book, I moved from a neighborhood in which I did not know anybody to one in which I know almost everybody. The reason for this is that my current house is part of a development that is designed in such a way that it is almost impossible not to come into contact with your neighbors. As a consequence of this, surplus food now flows much more freely in and out of my home. More generally, Chapter 7 argued that despite their instability; conduits that keep surplus food out of the waste stream can readily be identified. The challenge for policy makers here is to understand how, where, and when they are working (or not), and then develop ways to intensify and diffuse the practices that underpin their successful operation (see also Bulkeley and Gregson 2009). In order to do so, it will first be necessary to engage further with households along the lines set out in my suggestions for further research.

CLOSING REMARKS

It is hoped that this book has put forward an account of food waste that reaches beyond the common sense viewpoints that appear to inform popular and political thinking. The emphasis has been very much on bringing social scientific perspectives on home consumption, material culture and everyday life into closer dialogue with waste policy and research. Through ethnographic exploration of households, the research has engaged closely with the site at which current efforts to reduce food waste are currently focused and accordingly, I have made some effort to think about the practical implications of the account developed here. For as long as waste policy continues to focus its attention on households, I will continue to advocate the need for further empirical and social scientific research in the spirit of this book. As noted above, I imagine that these researches will be an essential prerequisite to the development of effective strategies for reducing food waste in households. To end, however, I wish to advocate a move away from the household. As Catherine Alexander and her colleagues (2013) point out, the extent to which policies are focussed on domestic waste reduction is disproportionate vis-à-vis overall levels of waste generation. That being so, the real challenge is one of reducing waste generation at other points in the food system. It follows that waste scholarship should look beyond the end of the pipe to engage with other sites and spaces of food waste generation and crucially— the connections between them. Only then will the generative potential of food waste, and its role in processes of cultural and economic organization come fully into view.

Notes

CHAPTER 1. BRINGING WASTE TO THE TABLE

1. Those who are not overly concerned with the historical development of waste scholarship can skip comfortably to the next section.

CHAPTER 2. ORDINARY DOMESTIC PRACTICE: CONCEPTUALIZING, RESEARCHING, REPRESENTING

1. http://ec.europa.eu/food/food/sustainability/causes_en.html (accessed February 19, 2013).
2. http://www.lovefoodhatewaste.com (accessed February 19, 2013).
3. Increasingly supermarkets in the U.K. are involved in campaigns to help their customers reduce the amount of food that they waste. For example in January 2013, Sainsbury's launched an active campaign in collaboration with WRAP that focussed on the Sunday roast in order to reduce household food waste.
4. To give another example, on March 5, 2013, Tristram Stuart tweeted: "Consumers are the sleeping giant in the #foodwaste equation. Public pressure will make food businesses across the board stop wasting food!"
5. See http://www.guardian.co.uk/environment/2013/feb/26/british-shoppers-irregular-fruit-vegetables (accessed July 8, 2013).
6. Incidentally, popular understandings of consumption—particularly those that find their way into food policy, cultural politics and environmental debate—tend to mirror, or perhaps derive from, the former and seem not to have caught up with the latter.
7. "Buy One Get One Free" offers.
8. In the interests of informed consent it was made perfectly clear to all respondents at the start of this research that ultimately, this is a study of food waste.
9. Not just by social scientists, but also engineers, policy makers, businesses, non-government organizations (NGOs) and activists.

10. Manchester is a city in the North West of England and is the third largest urban area in the United Kingdom.
11. As Sarah Pink (2004) points out, ethnographic research in the home is necessarily multi-sited, and certainly my own study of home consumption was not confined to the home. It will be recalled, for example, that this book started in the supermarket.
12. These are of course pseudonyms, as are all of the names used in the analysis.
13. Once respondents were recruited, they became very involved. I spent most of my time in these areas during the study and very often I would get a phone call inviting me to pop over or I would bump into participants in nearby shops, cafes and pubs. Participants told me that they enjoyed taking part in the study and as one respondent put it—they liked having somebody to carry their shopping!

CHAPTER 3. CONTEXTUALIZING HOUSEHOLD FOOD CONSUMPTION

1. For example a home-cooked meal is understood as proper food whereas a takeaway is not.
2. "Come Dine with Me" is a British game show in which four to five contestants compete for a cash prize. Each takes a turn to host a dinner party and the other competitors score their performance out of ten.
3. She likens herself to "one of those people that Jamie Oliver hates," referring to the despair that he displays when confronted with what he perceives as ignorance to "proper" food.
4. This is especially true to those provisioning food within a family context.
5. Everybody in this household has a "sweet tooth" but Kirsty has decided that they should only have a "sweet treat" once a day and where possible, that this should be fruit. Typically this is eaten after the evening meal but it is occasionally taken as a morning or mid-afternoon snack. In the instances where they have a cake or a chocolate bar instead of fruit, they either eat these items when they are "out and about" or make specific trips to the local convenience store if they are at home because Kirsty would rather not have them in the house "as a matter of course."
6. She suggests that this is because of the poor quality fruit available in the local corner shop and on one occasion when we were in there together, she points to it and asks if I thought anybody in their right mind would want to eat it. I agree that it looks less than appetizing.
7. However as the next chapter will demonstrate, these evaluations—and more besides—are actually incorporated into the practical routines of food provisioning that households develop.

8. The neighborhoods in which Rosewall Crescent and Leopold Lane are located are typical of the U.K. insofar as they are each served by one of the "big four" supermarkets (Tesco, Asda, Morrison's, Sainsbury's). These four supermarkets account for roughly 75 percent of the grocery market in the U.K. and their presence takes a number of forms, ranging from large out-of-town "super-stores" (to which people tend to drive) to smaller "convenience"-style outlets on the high street. Many of these stores have extended opening hours, including a number of "24 hour" options. Food is typically made available in pre-packaged quantities although there are moves towards having specialized "counters" for fish, meat, cheese and so on. "Loose" self-serve produce remains something of a rarity and when they are offered, there is almost always the option to put them straight into a plastic bag. There are a number of other supermarkets with a presence in the U.K. ranging from "no frills" to "high end"—the former are within easy reach of Leopold Lane and Rosewall Crescent, the latter are not. Both neighborhoods are served by a number of "local" and "corner" shops as well as being relatively close (c. 3 kilometers) to more affluent neighborhoods in which there are a number of delicatessens, independent stores and whole-food outlets. Throughout the study, the vast majority of grocery shopping was done at one of the "big four" supermarkets.

9. Iceland is a food retailer in the U.K. that specializes in low cost frozen foods. Its advertising slogan "... that's why mums go to Iceland" has been appropriated as ironic shorthand for being lazy in the kitchen.

CHAPTER 4. ANXIETY, ROUTINE AND OVER-PROVISIONING

1. http://england.lovefoodhatewaste.com/recipes?tid=All&tid_1=16&tid_2=177 (accessed July 10, 2013).

2. *Spaghetti alla puttanesca* translates literally as "whore's style spaghetti" and typically it is made with some combination of olive oil, garlic, tomatoes, olives, anchovies, capers, oregano, salt and pepper.

3. Single persons and younger couples without children were found to be slightly more erratic.

4. A colloquial term that is used in the U.K. to refer to a small, cheap café that specializes in fried and fast food.

5. It should be noted that although these routines typically evolved to cover a seven- to ten-day period, the fieldwork uncovered several instances of shorter intervals giving rise to a similar outcome. For example on one occasion, Chris and Faye—discussed in the following section—take advantage of a "2 for £5" deal on meat (one packet of pork loins, one packet of chicken wings) with the intention of using these as the basis for their meals on two consecutive

evenings. They eat the chicken wings as planned on the first night but an unexpected spell of warm weather leads them to the pub the following evening in order to "sit outside and make the most of the sun." After a few drinks they end up eating in the pub meaning that the pork loins that they had planned to eat become surplus to requirements.

6. In the U.K., large fridges and freezers—of the kind found in North America—are not commonplace. A typical fridge is 85cm (33.5 inches) high, up to 60cm (23.6 inches) wide, and up to 60cm (23.6 inches) deep. A fridge that is 130cm (51.2 inches) high is considered tall.

7. Miller's explication of thrift provides the basis for his aforementioned claims that consumption operates as a principal medium for constituting meaningful social relationships. For example, the careful management of household resources (saving) allows for future acts of consumption (spending), such as those undertaken by the mother who "keeps on searching until she finds the one article that satisfies this subtle and exacting need" when she is shopping for her child (see Chapter 2; see also Evans 2011b).

CHAPTER 5. THE GAP IN DISPOSAL: FROM SURPLUS TO EXCESS?

1. Edible in the sense that they could be used to prepare stock.
2. This list is indicative, not exhaustive.
3. All that was served was eaten. As Natalie points out: "I have teenage boys so clean plates aren't a problem in my house."
4. In the U.K., hair salons are traditionally closed on Mondays.
5. Conversely, the study also reveals instances in which, as the likelihood of an item being eaten diminishes, it gets buried further from view in the fridge.
6. Elsewhere in the study, food that followed this passage from the fridge into the freezer ended up in the bin. In these instances, surplus food became a casualty of "sorting the freezer out"—especially if households struggle to remember or recognize the item and fear that it might be unsafe as a result of being kept around for so long.
7. Kate and Louise were friends before moving into this house and tend to do most of their shopping together. Further, they are supporting one another in their efforts to "eat well" in preparation for the summer.
8. He also tells me that they would bring it up if it bothered them and cites an example of Kate "having a right go" at him when he had come home drunk one night and helped himself to one of the Weight Watchers cake bars that they had purchased. Later in the study, both Kate and Louise tell me that they are not really bothered by him eating their fruit as they find it quite amusing, and that they would rather he has it than for it to go in the bin.

9. She freezes leftover portions in a mixture of microwavable and oven-ready containers, and selects whichever option suits the duration of the visit. Microwaves are quicker but she prefers to use the oven when there is enough time.

10. To this I would add that the verb "to waste" could be applied to instances in which things are prematurely (i.e. before their sources of residual value have been exhausted) routed into the waste stream (see Evans 2012b).

CHAPTER 6. BINS AND THINGS

1. At the time of the study, neither street was subject to a zero tolerance policy for not recycling. In certain parts of the world (for example, areas of Japan and California), there are initiatives that use clear garbage bags in order to expose—and issue fines to—households that do not sort their trash appropriately. There are strong norms around recycling in the U.K. and as such, many households participate without the need for formal coercion.

2. See Kristeva (1982) and Warin (2010) on affectual responses to foodstuffs.

3. See Chapter 7 and the conclusion for discussion of the subtleties along the spectrum of food and non-food.

4. The analysis in Chapters 3 and 4 suggests that the provisioning of surplus is inconspicuously locked into patterns of household consumption meaning that the problem is not necessarily one that can be solved by consumers, nor is it one that is easily modified or readily amendable to conscious intervention.

5. At this point in the study, they had not been issued with a food-recycling bin. This came later—see below for a discussion of its effects on their domestic food waste practices.

6. In contrast, efforts to dispose of surplus food through alternative conduits are, as will be seen, fraught with all manner of difficulties.

7. A home that is owned and operated by a local authority.

8. The smaller receptacle takes up less space, is less of an affront to kitchen aesthetics and is emptied more frequently, meaning that households can participate in the initiative whilst still maintaining cleanliness, order, and hygiene in their home.

CHAPTER 7. GIFTING, RE-USE AND SALVAGE

1. Nigella Lawson—a high-profile celebrity chef whose cookery books and TV programmes play off the trope of the "domestic goddess."

2. She puts more effort in for special occasions, and when she has more time on her hands.

3. By which she means "unsophisticated shopping habits." "Scally" is a colloquial term that is roughly equivalent to the word "chavvy" (U.K.), "white trash"
(U.S.A.) or "bogan" (Australia/New Zealand).
4. It should of course be noted that the ever-present potential for "bad" (under-
cooked, gone off, triggering an allergic reaction or otherwise inappropriate) food
to make people ill is very often sufficient reason for not gifting surplus.
5. The same might be said of surplus allotment produce whether in the form of
"raw" fruit and vegetables, or pickles and preserves in hand-labeled jars.
6. More optimistically, Chapter 8 will consider some of the options that this opens
up in terms of thinking about initiatives for food waste reduction.
7. Boxed lunches that Japanese mothers prepare for their children.
8. See also the discussion of food recycling schemes in Chapter 6.
9. This is not to say that they are unimportant. To the contrary, they are funda-
mental and my hope is that this passing mention will spur some serious and
sustained scholarly engagement with the myriad questions that are thrown up
around the nexus of overconsumption, obesity, and waste.

CHAPTER 8. CONCLUSION: LIVING WITH FOOD, REDUCING WASTE

1. Following Latour (2005), I would rather view "the social" as that which is held
together by the assembly of humans and non-humans.
2. It is important to acknowledge that even so-called "alternative" models of
food production and distribution are culpable here. For example, just as supermarkets pre-package food in excessive quantities (see Chapter 4); so too are
Community Supported Agriculture (CSA) boxes overloaded with perishable
items that households might struggle to find a use for.
3. Thanks to Dr Tom Quested from WRAP for pointing this out to me.
4. I would rather label these as surplus prevention and surplus diversion
strategies.
5. This is already commonplace in parts of Asia.

Bibliography

Alexander, C., Gregson, N., and Gille, Z. (2013), "Food waste," in Murcott, A., Belasco, W., and Jackson, P. (eds) *The Handbook of Food Research*. London: Bloomsbury.

Allison, A. (1991), "Japanese mothers and obentōs: the lunch-box as ideological state apparatus." *Anthropological Quarterly* 64(4): 195–208.

Appadurai, A. (ed.) (1986), *The Social Life of Things: Commodities in Cultural Perspective*. Cambridge: Cambridge University Press.

Barnett, C., Cloke, P., Clarke, N., and Malpass, A. (2011), *Globalizing Responsibilities: The Political Rationalities of Ethical Consumption*. Oxford: Wiley-Blackwell.

Bataille, G. (1985) "The Notion of Expenditure," in A. Stoekl (ed.) *Visions of Excess: Selected Writings, 1927–1939*. Minneapolis: University of Minneapolis Press.

Bauman, Z. (2002), *Society under Siege*. Cambridge: Polity Press.

Beck, U. (1992), *Risk Society: Towards a New Modernity*. London: Sage.

Bennett, J. (2007), "Edible matter." *New Left Review* 45: 133–45.

—(2010), *Vibrant Matter: a Political Ecology of Things*. London: Duke University Press.

Bloom, J. (2010), *American Wasteland: How America Throws Away Nearly Half of Its Food (and What We Can Do About It)*. Cambridge, MA: DeCapo Press.

Bugge, A. and Almas, R. (2006), "Domestic dinner: representations and practices of a proper meal among young suburban mothers." *Journal of Consumer Culture* 6(2): 203–28.

Bulkeley, H. and Gregson, N. (2009), "Crossing the threshold: municipal waste policy and household waste generation." *Environment and Planning A* 41: 929–45.

Bulkeley, H., Watson, M., and Hudson, R. (2007). "Modes of governing municipal waste." *Environment and Planning A* 39: 2733–53.

Bullard, R. (1983), "Solid waste sites and the black Houston community." *Sociological Inquiry* 53 (2-3): 273–88.

Burridge, J. and Barker, J. (2009), "Food as a Medium for Emotional Management of the Family: Avoiding Complaint and Producing Love," in P. Jackson (ed.) *Changing Families, Changing Food*. Basingstoke: Palgrave Macmillan.

Cappellini, B. (2009), "The sacrifice of re-use: the travels of leftovers and family relations." *Journal of Consumer Behaviour* 8: 365–75.

Cappellini, B. and Parsons, E. (2013), "Practising thrift at dinnertime: mealtime leftovers, sacrifice and family membership." *The Sociological Review* 60(S2): 117–30.

Chappells, H. and Shove, E. (1999), "The dustbin: a study of domestic waste, household practices and utility services." *International Planning Studies* 4(2): 267–80.

Charles, N. and Kerr, M. (1988), *Women, Food and Families*. Manchester: Manchester University Press.

Cherrier, H. (2009), "Disposal and simple living: exploring the circulation of goods and the development of sacred consumption." *Journal of Consumer Behaviour* 8: 327–39.

Chilvers, J. and Burgess, J. (2008), "Power relations: the politics of risk and procedure in nuclear waste governance." *Environment and Planning A* 40: 1881–900.

Cieraad, I. (ed.) (1999), *At Home: An Anthropology of Domestic Space*. New York: Syracuse University Press.

Clarke, A. (2000), "Mother Swapping: The Trafficking of Nearly New Children's Wear," in P. Jackson, M. Lowe, D. Miller, and F. Mort (eds), *Commercial Cultures: Economies, Practices, Spaces*. Oxford: Berg, 23–46.

Coles, B. and Hallett, L. (2013), "Eating from the bin: salmon heads, waste and the markets that make them." *The Sociological Review* 60(S2): 156–73.

Cooper, T. (2005), "Slower Consumption: Reflections on Product Life Spans and the 'Throwaway Society'." *Journal of Industrial Ecology* 9(1): 51-67.

Crouch, D. and Ward, C. (1997), *The Allotment: its Landscape and Culture*. Nottingham: Five Leaves.

Davoudi, S. (2000), "Planning for waste management: changing discourses and institutional relationships," *Progress in Planning* 63: 165–216.

Dean, M. (1999), *Governmentality: Power and Rule in Modern Society*. London: Sage.

DeLillo, D. (1985) *White Noise*. London: Picador.

DeVault, M. (1991), *Feeding the Family: The Social Organization of Caring as Gendered Work*. Chicago, IL: Chicago University Press.

Douglas, M. (1966), *Purity and Danger*. London: Routledge.

—(1972), *Implicit Meanings*. London: Routledge.

Douny, L. (2007), "The materiality of domestic waste: the recycled cosmology of the Dogon of Malawi." *Journal of Material Culture* 12(3): 309–31.

Edwards, F. and Mercer, D. (2013), "Food waste in Australia: the freegan response." *The Sociological Review* 60(S2): 174–91.

Evans, D. (2011a), "Blaming the consumer – once again: the social and material contexts of everyday food waste practices in some English households." *Critical Public Health* 21(4): 429–40.

—(2011b), "Thrifty, green or frugal: reflections on sustainable consumption in a changing economic climate." *Geoforum* 42(5): 550–7.

—(2012a), "Beyond the throwaway society: ordinary domestic practice and a socio-logical approach to household food waste." *Sociology* 46(1): 43–58.

—(2012b), "Binning, gifting and recovery: the conduits of disposal in household food consumption." *Environment and Planning D: Society and Space* 30(6): 1123–37.

Evans, D., Campbell, H., and Murcott, A. (2013a), "A brief pre-history of food waste and the social sciences." *Sociological Review* 61(2): 1–22.

—(eds) (2013b), *Waste Matters: New Perspectives on Food and Society.* Oxford: Wiley-Blackwell.

Evans, D., Southerton, D., and McMeekin, A. (2012), "Sustainable Consumption, Behaviour Change Policies and Theories of Practice," in A. Warde and D. Southerton (eds) *The Habits of Consumption, COLLeGIUM: Studies across Disciplines in the Humanities and Social Sciences.* Helsinki: Helsinki Collegium for Advanced Studies 12: 113–29.

Fine, B. (1995), "From political economy to consumption," in D. Miller (ed.) *Acknowledging Consumption.* London: Routledge.

Fine, G. (1996), *Kitchens: the Culture of Restaurant Work.* Berkeley and Los Angeles: University of California Press.

Fischer, E. and Benson, P. (2006), *Broccoli and Desire: Global Connections and Maya Struggles in Postwar Guatemala.* California: Stanford University Press.

Food and Agriculture Organization of the United Nations (FAO) (2011), *Global Food Losses and Food Waste: Extent, Causes and Prevention.* Rome: Food and Agriculture Organization of the United Nations.

—(2012), *The State of Food Insecurity in the World.* Rome: Food and Agriculture Organization of the United Nations.

Freidberg, S. (2009), *Fresh: A Perishable History.* Cambridge, MA: Harvard University Press.

Giddens, A. (1984), *The Constitution of Society.* Cambridge: Polity Press.

Gille, Z. (2007), *From the Cult of Waste to the Trash Heap of History: The Politics of Waste in Socialist and Postsocialist Hungary.* Bloomington, IN: University of Indiana Press.

—(2010), "Actor networks, modes of production, and waste regimes: reassembling the macro-social." *Environment and Planning A* 42(5): 1049–64.

—(2013), "From risk to waste: Global food waste regimes." *The Sociological Review* 60(S2): 23–42.

Goody, J. (1982), *Cooking, Cuisine and Class: A Study in Comparative Sociology.* Cambridge: Cambridge University Press.

Gregson, N., (2007), *Living with Things: Ridding, Accommodation, Dwelling.* Oxford: Sean Kingston Publishing.

Gregson, N. and Crang, M. (2010), "Guest Editorial." *Environment and Planning A* 42: 1026–1032.

Gregson, N., Crang, M., Ahamed, F., Akter, N., and Ferdous, R. (2010), "Following things of rubbish value: end-of-life ships, 'chock-chocky' furniture and the Bangladeshi middle class consumer." *Geoforum* 41: 846–54.

Gregson, N. and Crewe, L. (2003), *Second Hand Cultures*. Oxford: Berg.

Gregson, N., Metcalfe, A., and Crewe, L. (2007a), "Identity, Mobility, and the Throwaway Society." *Environment and Planning D: Society and Space* 25: 682–700.

—(2007b), "Moving things along: the conduits and practices of divestment in consumption." *Transactions of the Institute of British Geographers* 32(2): 187–200.

Gregson, N., Watkins, H., and Calestani, M. (2010), "Inextinguishable fibres: demolition and the vital materialisms of asbestos." *Environment and Planning A* 42: 1065–83.

Gronow, J. and Warde, A. (eds) (2001), *Ordinary Consumption*. London: Routledge.

Halkier, B. (2009), "Suitable cooking? performance and positionings in cooking practices among Danish women." *Food, Culture and Society* 12(3): 357–77.

Hawkins, G. (2006), *The Ethics of Waste: How we Relate to Rubbish*, Lanham: Rowman and Littlefield.

—(2013), "The performativity of food packaging: market devices, waste crisis and recycling." *The Sociological Review* 60(S2): 66–83.

Heiman, M. (1996), "Race, class and waste: new perspectives on environmental justice." *Antipode* 28(2): 111–21.

Hertz, R. (1960), "A Contribution to the Study of Collective Representation of Death," in R. Needham and C. Needham (trans.) *Death and the Right Hand*, 27–86. London: Cohen and West.

Hetherington, K. (2004), "Secondhandedness: consumption, disposal and absent presence." *Environment and Planning D: Society and Space* 22: 157–73.

Ingold, T. (2007), "Materials against materiality." *Archaeological Dialogues* 14(1): 1–16.

Institution of Mechanical Engineers (ImechE) (2013), *Global Food: Waste Not, Want Not*. London: Institution of Mechanical Engineers.

Jackson, P. (ed.) (2009), *Changing Families, Changing Food*. Basingstoke: Palgrave Macmillan.

Jackson, P. and Everts, J. (2010), "Anxiety and social practice." *Environment and Planning A* 42: 2791–806.

Jackson, P., Watson, M. and Piper, N. (2013), "Locating anxiety in the social: the cultural mediation of food fears." *European Journal of Cultural Studies* 16: 24–42.

James, A. Kjorhol, A., and Vebjorg, T. (eds) (2009), *Children, Food and Identity in Everyday Life*. Basingstoke: Palgrave Macmillan.

Koch, S. (2012), *A Theory of Grocery Shopping: Food, Choice and Conflict*. Oxford: Berg.

Kopytoff, I. (1986), "The Cultural Biography of Things: Commodification as a Process," in A. Appadurai (ed.) *The Social Life of Things: Commodities in Cultural Perspective*. Cambridge: Cambridge University Press, 64–94.

Kristeva, J. (1982), *The Powers of Horror: An Essay on Abjection*. New York: Colombia University Press.

Krzywoszynska, A. (2013), "'Waste? you mean by-products!' from bio-waste management to agro-ecology in Italian winemaking and beyond." *The Sociological Review* 60(S2): 47–65.

Kusenbach, M. (2003), "Street phenomenology: the go-along as ethnographic research tool." *Ethnography* 4(3): 455–85.

Laporte, D. (1999), *A History of Shit*. Cambridge, MA: MIT Press.

Lasch, S. and Lury, C. (1996), *Global Cultural Industries: the Mediation of Things*. Cambridge: Polity.

Latour, B. (2005), *Reassembling the Social: An Introduction to Actor-Network-Theory*. Oxford: Oxford University Press.

Lévi-Strauss, C. (1966), "The culinary triangle." *New Society* 16(6): 937–40.

Littler, J. (2009), *Radical Consumption: Shopping for Change in Contemporary Culture*. Berkshire: Open University Press.

Lockie, S. (2002) "The invisible mouth: mobilizing the consumer in food consumption networks." *Sociologia Ruralis* 42(4): 278–94.

Lucas, G. (2002), "Disposability and dispossession in the twentieth century." *Journal of Material Culture* 7: 5–22.

Lupton, D. (1996), *Food, the Body and the Self*. London: Sage.

Malinowski, B. (1922), *The Argonauts of the Western Pacific: An Account of Native Enterprise and Adventure in the Archipelagoes of Melanesian New Guinea*. London: Routledge.

Marcus, G. (1995), "Ethnography in/of the world system: the emergence of multi-sited ethnography." *Annual Review of Anthropology* 24: 95–117.

Martuzzi, M., Mitis, F., and Forastiere, F. (2010), "Inequalities, inequities, environmental justice in waste management and health." *European Journal of Public Health* 20(1): 22–6.

Mauss, M. (1954), *The Gift: Forms and Function of Exchange in Archaic Societies*. London: Cohen and West.

Meagher, S. (2010), "Critical thinking about the right to the city: mapping garbage routes." *City: Analysis of Urban Trends, Culture, Theory, Policy, Action* 14(4): 427–33.

Meah, A. and Watson, M. (2011), "Saints and slackers: challenging discourses about the decline of domestic cooking." *Sociological Research Online* 16(2): 6.

Melosi, A. (2004), *Garbage in the Cities: Refuse, Reform, and the Environment* (rev. edn). Pittsburgh: University of Pittsburgh Press.

Metcalfe, A., Riley, M., Barr, S., Tudor, T., Robinson, G., and Gilbert, S. (2013), "Food waste bins: bridging infrastructures and practices." *The Sociological Review* 60(S2): 135–55.

Micheletti, M. (2003), *Political Virtue and Shopping: Individuals, Consumerism and Collective Action*. London: Routledge.

Miller, D. (1988), "Appropriating the state on a council estate." *Man* 23: 353–72.

—(1995), "Consumption as the Vanguard of History," in D. Miller (ed.) *Acknowledging Consumption*. London: Routledge.

—(1998), *A Theory of Shopping*. Cambridge: Polity Press.

—(2001a), *Home Possessions*. Oxford: Berg.

—(2001b), "The poverty of morality." *Journal of Consumer Culture* 1(2): 225–43.

—(2008), *The Comfort of Things*. Cambridge: Polity Press.

Milne, R. (2013), "Arbiters of waste: date labels, the consumer and knowing good, safe food." *The Sociological Review* 60(S2): 84–101.

Milne, R., Wenzer, J., Brembeck, H., and Brodin, M. (2011), "Fraught cuisine: food scares and the modulation of anxieties." *Distinktion: Scandinavian Journal of Social Theory* 12(2): 177–92.

Mitchell, J. (1999), "The British main meal in the 1990s: has it changed its identity?" *British Food Journal* 101(11): 871–83.

Munro, R. (1983), "It's a Pleasure to Cook for Him: Food, Mealtimes and Gender in Some South Wales Households," in E. Garmarnikow (ed.) *The Public and the Private*. London: Heinemann.

—(1993), "Talking of good food: an empirical study of women's conceptualisations." *Food and Foodways* 5(3): 305–18.

—(1995), "The Disposal of the Meal," in D. Marshall (ed.) *Food Choice and the Consumer*. London: Blackie.

—(2013), "The disposal of place: facing modernity in the kitchen-diner." *The Sociological Review* 60(S2): 212–31.

Murcott, A. (1995), "Social influences on food choice and dietary change: a socio-logical attitude." *Proceedings of the Nutrition Society*, 54: 729–35.

—(1997), "Family Meals – a Thing of the Past?," in P. Caplan (ed.) *Food, Health and Identity*. London: Routledge.

—(2002), "Nutrition and inequalities: a note on sociological approaches." *European Journal of Public Health* 12: 203–7.

Norris, L. (2004), "Shedding skins: the materiality of divestment in India." *Journal of Material Culture* 9(1): 59–71.

Norris, P. (2007), "Political participation," in C. Boix and S. Stokes (eds) *The Oxford Handbook of Comparative Politics*. Oxford: Oxford University Press.

Oakley, A. (1974), *The Sociology of Housework*. Oxford: Blackwell.

O'Brien, M. (2007), *A Crisis of Waste? Understanding the Rubbish Society*. London and New York: Routledge.

—(2013), "A 'lasting transformation' of capitalist surplus: from food stocks to feedstocks." *The Sociological Review* 60(S2): 192–211.

Olsen, B. (2010), *In Defence of Things: Archaeology and the Ontology of Objects*. Plymouth: Rowman and Littlefield.

Packard, V. (1961), *The Waste Makers*. London: Longman.

Peterson, A., Davis, M., Fraser, S., and Lindsay, J. (2010), "Healthy living and citizenship: an overview." *Critical Public Health* 20(4): 391–400.

Petts, J. (2004), "Barriers to participation and deliberation in risk decisions: evidence from waste management." *Journal of Risk Research* 7(2): 115–33.

Pink, S. (2004), *Home Truths: Gender, Domestic Objects and Everyday Life.* Oxford: Berg.

—(2012), *Situating Everyday Life: Practices and Places.* London: Sage.

Quested, T., Marsh, E., Stunell, D., and Parry, A. (2013), "Spaghetti soup: the complex world of food waste behaviours." *Journal of Resources, Conservation and Recycling* 79: 43–51.

Rathje, W. and Murphy, C. (1992), *Rubbish: The Archaeology of Garbage.* New York: HarperCollins.

Reckwitz, A. (2002), "Towards a theory of social practices: a development in culturalist theorizing." *European Journal of Social Theory* 5: 243–63.

Redclift, M. (1996), *Wasted: Counting the Costs of Global Consumption.* London: Earthscan.

Reno, J. (2009), "Your trash is someone else's treasure: the politics of value at a Michigan landfill." *Journal of Material Culture* 14(1): 29–46.

Rose, N. (1999), *Powers of Freedom.* Cambridge: Cambridge University Press.

Scanlan, J. (2005), *On Garbage.* London: Reaktion Books.

Schatzki, T. (1996), *Social Practices.* Cambridge: Cambridge University Press.

Schatzki, T., Knorr-Cetina, K., and von Savigny, E. (2001), *The Practice Turn in Contemporary Theory.* London: Routledge.

Schor, J. (1998), *The Overspent American: Upscaling, Downshifting and the New Consumer.* New York: Basic Books.

Schrift, A. (ed.) (1997), *The Logic of the Gift: Toward an Ethic of Generosity.* London and New York: Routledge.

Short, F. (2006), *Kitchen Secrets: The Meaning of Cooking in Everyday Life.* Oxford: Berg.

Shove, E. (2003), *Comfort, Cleanliness and Convenience – the Social Organisation of Normality.* Oxford: Berg.

—(2010), "Beyond the ABC: climate change policy and theories of social change." *Environment and Planning A* 42(6): 1273–85.

Shove, E. and Pantzar, M. (2005), "Consumers, producers and practices: understanding the invention and reinvention of Nordic walking." *Journal of Consumer Culture,* 5: 43–64.

Shove, E., Pantzar, M., and Watson, M. (2012), *The Dynamics of Social Practice: Everyday Life and how it Changes.* London: Sage.

Shove, E. and Southerton, D. (2000) "Defrosting the freezer: from novelty to convenience: a narrative of normalization." *Journal of Material Culture* 5: 301–19.

Shove, E. and Warde, A. (2002), "Inconspicuous Consumption: The Sociology of Lifestyles, Consumption and the Environment," in R. Dunlap, F. Buttel, P. Dickens, and A. Gijswijt (eds) *Sociological Theory and the Environment:*

Classical Foundations, Contemporary Insights. New York and Oxford: Rowman and Littlefield, 230–52.

Silva, E. (2010), *Technology, Culture, Family: Influences on Home Life.* Basingstoke: Palgrave Macmillan.

Southerton, D. (2001), "Consuming kitchens: taste, context and identity formation." *Journal of Consumer Culture* 1(2): 179–203.

—(2003), "Squeezing time: allocating practices, coordinating networks and scheduling society." *Time and Society* 12(1): 5–25.

—(2013), "Habits, routines and temporalities of consumption: from individual behaviours to the reproduction of everyday practices." *Time and Society.* 22(3): 335–55.

Spaargaren, G., Oosterveer, P., and Loeber, A. (eds) (2012), *Food Practices in Transition: Changing Food Consumption, Retail and Production in the Age of Reflexive Modernity.* London: Routledge.

Strasser, S. (1999), *Waste and Want: The Social History of Trash.* London: Metropolitan Books.

Stuart, T. (2009), *Waste: Uncovering the Global Food Scandal.* New York: W. W. Norton.

Thompson, M. (1979), *Rubbish Theory: The Creation and Destruction of Value.* Oxford: Oxford University Press.

Van Loon, J. (2002), *Risk and Technological Culture: Towards a Sociology of Virulence.* Oxford: Routledge.

Warde, A. (1997), *Consumption, Food and Taste.* Cambridge: Polity Press.

—(1999), "Convenience food: space and timing." *British Food Journal* 101(7): 518–27.

—(2005), "Consumption and theories of practice." *Journal of Consumer Culture,* 5(2): 131–53.

Warin, M. (2010), *Abject Relations: Everyday Worlds of Anorexia.* New Brunswick: Rutgers University Press.

Watkins, H. (2006), "Beauty queen, bulletin board and browser: rescripting the refrigerator gender." *Place and Culture* 13(2): 143–52.

Watson, M. and Meah, A. (2013), "Food, waste and safety: negotiating conflicting social anxieties into the practices of domestic provisioning." *The Sociological Review* 60(S2): 98–116.

Wilkinson, I. (2001), *Anxiety in a Risk Society.* London: Routledge.

WRAP (2011), *New Estimates for Household Food and Drink Waste in the UK.* Banbury: Waste and Resources Action Programme.

Index